THE END TIMES

What You Haven't Been Told

J. Martin Davis

PUBLISHED BY
KWP PUBLISHING COMPANY
AN IMPRINT OF KINGDOM WORD PUBLICATIONS
ALBION, MICHIGAN 49224

Printed in the U.S.A

THE END TIMES
What You Haven't Been Told

ISBN 978-0-9712916-8-3
Library of Congress Control Number 2010932629

Unless otherwise noted, all scripture references are taken from the New King James Version of the Bible.

Cover Design **WRITERIGHT PUBLISHING SERVICES**
Professional Copy Edit Services by **KINGDOMSCRIBE SERVICES**

TABLE OF CONTENTS

Dedication

This book is dedicated to my father. He was the best Bible scholar I have ever known. He didn't answer questions up front. If you asked him a question, he gave you scripture and let you decide the answer for yourself.

I was sitting in one of his bible classes when a middle aged man asked a question that I thought wow, that's a tough one. My dad's response was, 'That's an easy one'. He went on to explain it in a way everyone there could understand.

On another occasion the minister at his church preached on some events from the Old Testament. After the service was over and no one else was around, my father went to the minister and explained to him, he had connected a couple events together that in fact were separated by many months and were not connected.

He encouraged me to undertake this study and to have it published. It is with his dedication to detail I have taken this on.

Preface

I am a born again Christian that believes the bible is the inerrant word of God.

Up front I want to say this book is not intended to be evangelistic or denominational. It is intended to be a clarification of what the King James Bible says. This study was done with a King James Bible and a Strong's Concordance. The scriptures were cut and pasted from 'bible.com'.

Every statement of fact is backed up by scripture taken in context and is consistent with other scriptures. The bible doesn't lie and it does not conflict itself.

Some of the controversial topics covered are:

- Once saved always saved
- Absent from the body present with the lord
- Who goes to heaven and when
- When is the Rapture
- The chronology of the Book of Revelations
- Are the Great Tribulation and the Wrath of God the same thing
- When is Armageddon
- Who goes to the Great White Throne Judgment
- Who goes thru the Millennium

I don't pretend to have all the answers. Where there doesn't appear to be a scriptural answer I say so. In some cases I give a hypothetical analysis and I tell you it is a guess.

This study of the end times does not cover chapter and verse of the end times scriptures. Areas that are not controversial are not covered in detail.

I believe when we approach the time of the Great Tribulation we will be able to understand the whole prophecy concerning the end times. Until then, we can only guess what some of the prophecy actually means. Such questions as who will be the 10 nations of the beast? Who will be the antichrist? Who will be the false prophet? What are the Locusts with the sting in their tail? We have many, many questions we can not answer.

Chapter 1 An Overview of the End Times

Preface

This chapter encompasses the entire end time analysis without the documentation. Please do not jump to any conclusions until you have read the documented portions. There are areas where you are going to hear things you have never heard before; or you will be hearing them from a different point of view. In any case, what you read here is documented unless otherwise stated. There are some areas where I will tell you there just isn't enough information to make a definitive conclusion. In some cases; I give a possibility of what happens, but I'll tell you it is my own guess.

CHRONOLOGY

When John received this series of revelations, he was imprisoned on the Isle of Patmos. It is located about 60 miles southwest of Ephesus in the Aegean Sea. It is believed John was imprisoned there by Domitian, Emperor of Rome A.D. 81-96. (Titus Flavius Domitianus)

The Book of the Revelation is not a chronological account. Most history books start at a point in time and then proceed forward. The Book of the Revelation is not a history book. It is a book of prophecy written down by John after he had received the revelation. Apparently, John wrote the 'book' as he recalled what he had seen. It is not sequential. The book tells of different events that happen at the same point in time, but in separate chapters. By the time you've read this entire book, you will know there is very little of the Book of the Revelation that is sequential. It is not my intent in writing this book to give a verse-by-verse explanation of each little detail. Rather, I hope to give a good understanding of the end time major events and the major players. My goal is to straighten out some misconceptions of the timing of certain events and to add some overlooked events.

For example:

There are at least six different sequences in the Book of the Revelation that lead to Armageddon. Most of these six sequences happen at the same time. Most end time writers try to make them sequential.

There is one chapter that repeats the same basic information three separate times.

When was the last time you heard there are non-Christian nations that will continue through the Millennium?

Did you know John was told to prophesy 'again' in the middle of this Book of the Revelation after he had revealed most of the Tribulation?

There are several things in the Book of the Revelation I had never heard before. We will reveal more as we go.

UNDERSTANDING TIME REFERENCES

Before we go any further I need to explain some of the references to time in end time prophecy. There are several different references to time measurement in end time prophecy. The most common ones are

3-1/2 years, 1260 days, 42 months, 70 weeks, times, time and Half (1/2) time (or dividing of time). Let's look at each one individually.

One week refers to seven years. One week would then represent seven years. Seventy weeks would represent 490 years.

The term 'time' refers to one year. 'Times' would represent two years. Half (1/2) time would represent ½ year.

So, Times (2 years) + Time (1 year) + ½ Time (½ year) = 3-1/2 years.

In the Jewish calendar, a 'month' is 30 days.

1260 days = 42 months = 3-1/2 years.

Twelve-hundred sixty days is the accepted length of the Tribulation period. This is the time the antichrist will be given to do his thing. It is the amount of time the two witnesses will have to testify to the whole world.

We will cover more times later on in our study.

TECHNICAL LANGUAGE AND UNDERSTANDING

The other area of complication is the technical knowledge of the author. Never have I heard about the fact, John is trying to relate events (visions) scheduled to happen at least 2,000 years into his future. He doesn't appear to have been given the technical comprehension of what he is trying to relate. Consequently, his vocabulary is limited to the era he lived in. For example, what is a flying horse with power in its tail and in its nose? It sends out fire and brimstone and smoke.

There are several places in Scripture where conveyances are described in ways that would lead you to believe they are more technologically advanced than the language of the day could adequately describe. In Daniel 12:4, Daniel is told by an angel, " [4]*But thou, O Daniel, shut up the words, and seal the book, even to the time of the end: many shall run to and fro, and knowledge shall be increased*". This is significant. The technological advancements and a fuller understanding of history and its application to Scripture increase as time goes on. Simply put, as time progresses the prophecies of the 'sealed up book' will be easier to understand. I believe the people around at the end time will be able to fully understand the prophecy. We know some now and we will know more as time goes on. For now, we can only speculate on some of what we read.

These next two Scriptures depict what I am talking about as regards to vocabulary and a technical knowledge unable to adequately describe what the writer is trying to describe. The first is the ascension of Elijah in the presence of Elisha. The second is an encounter with a conveyance with four creatures inside. I do not intend to try to explain either one. I am just using them to show how inadequate biblical terminology and technical understanding can be. It isn't just an end time thing.

> 2Kings 2:11 [11]*And it came to pass, as they still went on, and talked, that, behold, there appeared* **a chariot of fire**, *and horses of fire, and parted them both asunder; and Elijah went up by a whirlwind into heaven.*
>
> *In Ezekiel 1: 5-28, [5]Also out of the midst thereof came the likeness of four living creatures. And this was their appearance; they had the likeness of a man. [6]And every one had four faces, and every one had four wings. [7]And their feet were straight feet; and the sole of their feet was like the sole of a*

calf's foot: and they sparkled like the colour of burnished brass. [8]And
they had the hands of a man under their wings on their four sides; and
they four had their faces and their wings. [9]Their wings were joined one to
another; they turned not when they went; they went every one straight
forward. [10]As for the likeness of their faces, they four had the face of a
man, and the face of a lion, on the right side: and they four had the face of
an ox on the left side; they four also had the face of an eagle. [11]Thus were
their faces: and their wings were stretched upward; two wings of every
one were joined one to another, and two covered their bodies. [12]And they
went every one straight forward: whither the spirit was to go, they went;
and they turned not when they went. [13]As for the likeness of the living
creatures, their appearance was like burning coals of fire, and like the
appearance of lamps: it went up and down among the living creatures;
and the fire was bright, and out of the fire went forth lightning. [14]And the
living creatures ran and returned as the appearance of a flash of
lightning. [15]Now as I beheld the living creatures, behold one wheel upon
the earth by the living creatures, with his four faces. [16]The appearance of
the wheels and their work was like unto the colour of a beryl: and they
four had one likeness: and their appearance and their work was as it were
a wheel in the middle of a wheel. [17]When they went, they went upon their
four sides: and they turned not when they went. [18]As for their rings, they
were so high that they were dreadful; and their rings were full of eyes
round about them four. [19]And when the living creatures went, the wheels
went by them: and when the living creatures were lifted up from the earth,
the wheels were lifted up. [20]Whithersoever the spirit was to go, they went,
thither was their spirit to go; and the wheels were lifted up over against
them: for the spirit of the living creature was in the wheels. [21]When those
went, these went; and when those stood, these stood; and when those were

lifted up from the earth, the wheels were lifted up over against them: for the spirit of the living creature was in the wheels. [22]And the likeness of the firmament upon the heads of the living creature was as the colour of the terrible crystal, stretched forth over their heads above. [23]And under the firmament were their wings straight, the one toward the other: every one had two, which covered on this side, and every one had two, which covered on that side, their bodies. [24]And when they went, I heard the noise of their wings, like the noise of great waters, as the voice of the Almighty, the voice of speech, as the noise of an host: when they stood, they let down their wings. [25]And there was a voice from the firmament that was over their heads, when they stood, and had let down their wings. [26]And above the firmament that was over their heads was the likeness of a throne, as the appearance of a sapphire stone: and upon the likeness of the throne was the likeness as the appearance of a man above upon it. [27]And I saw as the colour of amber, as the appearance of fire round about within it, from the appearance of his loins even upward, and from the appearance of his loins even downward, I saw as it were the appearance of fire, and it had brightness round about. [28]As the appearance of the bow that is in the cloud in the day of rain, so was the appearance of the brightness round about. This was the appearance of the likeness of the glory of the LORD. And when I saw it, I fell upon my face, and I heard a voice of one that spake.

END TIMES OUTLINE BY JESUS CHRIST

We are lucky to have been given one of the best guides to the end times, by Jesus Christ.

In Matthew 24, Jesus was speaking to His apostles and He gave them a coarse outline of the events that were to come.

There are a couple of items in Jesus' outline I would like to expound upon.

In verse 1 He says, "*....he that shall endure* **unto the end***, the same shall be saved.*" This Scripture is not adequately explained from the pulpit. We hear the Lord is coming soon. But they don't explain how they can say that. Yes, the Lord could come in the clouds, but not as soon as some might think. The real reason they can say the Lord is coming soon is you may die at anytime. When you die, it becomes your end time. It ultimately leads to your rapture.

In verse 14 Jesus says, "*....this gospel of the kingdom shall be preached in all the world for a witness unto all nations; and* **then shall the end come***.*"

This is also referred to in Chapter 14 of the Book of the Revelation and then couple this with God's two witnesses in Chapter 11 of the Book of the Revelation and you can clearly see the preaching of the gospel to the whole world doesn't end until the end of the Tribulation period. God sends His two witnesses specifically to *prophesy a thousand two hundred and threescore days* and *Jesus is the spirit of prophecy.* The spreading of the everlasting gospel (the testimony of Jesus Christ) *to every nation, tribe, tongue, and people* will continue until the end of the Great Tribulation period.

PRE-TRIBULATION

After thousands of years of wars, famines, pestilences, and false teachers, the end time will come and bring a time of tribulation such as has never been seen before.

There are many questions that come to mind:

1. What will be different during the Great Tribulation period?
2. How will we know when the end times are here?
3. Will we be able to tell when the end times are here?
4. Will we be able to know when the Great Tribulation has started or is about to start.
5. Will we be able to know when the Great Tribulation is about to end?

These are all good and legitimate questions. In this book we will answer all of these questions and you will know and will be able to understand the answers.

Before the Tribulation begins, there will be a new worldwide empire come to power. Initially it will be a ten-nation coalition. Then a leader will take over three of those nations and then will move to take over leadership of the ten- nation coalition, and eventually become ruler of the world. He will be joined by a religious leader. This religious leader will come out of the old Medo-Persian Empire. He most likely will be a Muslim cleric.

As a side note, Islam teaches there will be a 12th Imam who will come to rule over a Muslim world at the end times. They believe he will return just before the end of the world. His appearance will be preceded by a number of prophetic events during 3 years of horrendous world chaos, tyranny and oppression. They believe he will then rule over the Arab nations for seven years. They believe he will eradicate all tyranny and oppression, bringing harmony and total peace (a man of peace). And to top it all, he will lead a prayer in Mecca, at which Jesus will be at his side and follow in.

If all of this is true, the false prophet cannot be the 12th Imam. The 12th Imam won't come to power until there has been tribulation for 3 years (1080 days). In Bible prophecy that would be 6 months before the end of the Great Tribulation. The false prophet has to have been around longer than that to do all he has to do in Bible prophecy.

There is a great significance to having a coalition of power between a non-Arab (the antichrist) and an Arab religious leader (false prophet). The combination would allow the empire to promise and deliver global peace at least temporarily.

As a symbol of his power, the antichrist will negotiate a Seven-year treaty with Israel. It will be to guarantee peace and safety for the nation of Israel and its neighbors. After 3-1/2 years the antichrist and the false prophet will have cemented their power around the world, and they will break the Seven-year treaty at its midpoint. This will signal the beginning of the Great Tribulation.

Now, when people tell you there is no way to know when the Tribulation will start, you can tell them the truth.

First, you have the rise of a ten-nation coalition. There will be a single leader emerge in that government. Eventually, he will blaspheme God and encourage satanic worship and a culture of sin. In the mean time, he will be joined by a ruler of Arab descent. Then, there will be a Seven-year treaty signed with Israel. As you begin to see these events come to pass, you can be pretty sure its time. When the Treaty is broken at three and half years, you will know for sure the end is at hand. That will leave 3-1/2 years (1260 days, 42 months, or times time and half time) until the end of the Great Tribulation.

The key is the Seven-year treaty. The Great Tribulation can't start until three and half years after the signing of the Seven-year Treaty.

Armageddon and the second coming of Jesus Christ can't be until seven years after the signing of the Seven-year treaty. So, if someone tells you the Tribulation could start tomorrow, you will know the right question. Was the Seven-year treaty signed three and a half years ago?

THE GREAT TRIBULATION

What is the Great Tribulation? Whom does it affect? Simply put, it is the systematic removal of all professing Jews and Christians from the face of the earth. If you are here on earth at that time and maintain your testimony of salvation through Jesus Christ, you most likely will be killed. The antichrist will demand everyone expose (betray) anyone they know to be a professing Christian. Jesus told His disciples, "*And then shall many be offended, and shall betray one another, and shall hate one another (Matthew 24:10).*" It could be family members, coworkers, anyone. Initially the persecution and killings will be in Israel. But the push from Satan will require the blood of all saints, no matter where they live.

Here again the connection of a Muslim cleric as second seat in the new world government makes even more sense. We have all seen the effects of Shariah Law in recent times. When a Muslim becomes involved with or converts to Christianity, it means death to the infidel. During the Tribulation this practice will be expanded to all Christians. The betrayer may be your brother, sister, mother, father, friend, coworker. It could be anyone. To the hard core Muslim, all non-Muslims must die or be converted. Under the antichrist, all Christians must renounce their faith or die.

As a part of this power trip by the antichrist and the false prophet, everyone will be required to worship the antichrist as a deity. If you don't, you die. One of the ways they will have you show your loyalty to the antichrist will be to have you receive a mark on your right hand or on your forehead. The mark has great significance. You won't be able to buy or sell anything without it. No groceries, no gas for your car, no electricity for your house, etc. This mark will probably be the result of the implanting of a microchip under the skin. We have dogs being implanted with a chip for identification in today's world. Also, there is discussion of injecting every one with a medical chip that can be updated every time you go to a doctor. Today we have pass cards being used as security at various businesses. If you have the card in your pocket or purse, the scanner can sense it and allow you access. I can envision the mark of the beast being used in the same way. It will identify who you are. It could be used like a transponder on airplanes or like OnStar in GM cars and trucks. It could be used to track exactly where you are. It could also have your medical records it. The main control is your inability to purchase goods and services. It will be your credit/debit card. There will be no money, no other way to make purchases at a grocery store or gas station, etc. The only way to buy or sell anything will be with the mark of the beast. Those without the mark will have to rely on one another.

They will have to use good old fashion bartering and work exchange. This mark will probably seem like a natural and easy progression from the current system of the day. I don't plan to accept any of it.

The inability to buy and sell without the mark would be bad enough, but God has put out another outcome for receiving the mark and worshipping the Beast. God has promised, if any of us receive the mark and worship the beast, we will be eternally damned. That doesn't sound like a promise I want kept. God also let it be known those who do not receive the mark and do not worship the beast will live and reign with Him a thousand years. Wow, that's the group I want to be in. A thousand years with Jesus Christ sounds good to me.

TWO WITNESSES

We have been told the gospel must be preached to the entire world before the Tribulation. Apparently this isn't the case. The gospel will be preached throughout the entire Tribulation period.

God tells us He is going to place His two witnesses in Jerusalem to prophesy 1260 days (3-1/2 years). They will be humbly dressed. They won't be attending any state balls or victory celebrations. They will be testifying of Jesus Christ, much the same as John the Baptist did over two thousand years ago. Even though they will live in Israel, I don't believe they will be testifying to Israel only. I believe they will be testifying to the whole world by way of radio and television.

During their time on earth, the two witnesses will have powers. They will be able to defend themselves against physical attacks by a fire that proceeds from their mouth. I don't have an explanation of what this really is, or how it will work. That forces me back to 'if God said it, I believe it.'

The two witnesses will have other powers as well. We are told they will possess the power over the same plagues used by Moses to encourage Egypt to let God's people go. They will be able to turn water to blood, to stop the rain, to bring on pestilences, etc.

At the end of the 1260 days the antichrist will kill them and let them lay in the streets for the whole world to see and to glory in his power. Then, on the third day God will breathe life back into them and they will stand erect, scaring everyone who sees them. Then God will take His two witnesses back to Heaven in preparation for His triumphant return. Their enemies will be watching as they are '*...ascended up to heaven in a cloud (Revelation 11:12)*'. Does this sound familiar? On the third day they are resurrected and ascend to Heaven on a cloud. I believe this will be the time of the Rapture as well.

Then within an hour there will be a great earthquake. So great an earthquake a tenth of the city will fall, and seven thousand men will be killed.

SAINTS IN HEAVEN

John was given visions of saints in Heaven at various points during the Great Tribulation. He was also given a vision of the 144,000 Jews who have kept themselves pure. There are 12,000 from each of the tribes of Israel. There is none from the tribe of Dan. Instead there are 12,000 from the tribe of Manassas. The tribe of Dan was excluded and replaced by the tribe of Manassas because the tribe of Dan had turned to idol worship.

When John was first in Heaven, the only saints he reported seeing were twenty-four elders. There was no mention of any multitude or even a few saints from earth, other than the twenty-four elders.

After the first four seals of the Book of Seals have been opened, he sees more saints in Heaven. He saw the souls of saints killed for their belief in God. These are saints killed in the Tribulation. They are to wait until their fellow saints are killed 'who should be killed as they were'. We aren't given an indication of the number of them at this time. However, as we will see in the next vision there are a lot more to come.

Then John is given another vision of the saints in Heaven. This time there are a few more. In fact, there is a great multitude, which no man could number, of all nations, and kindred, and people, and tongues. John is told by an angel '... *these are they which came out of great tribulation, and have washed their robes, and made them white in the blood of the Lamb (Revelation 7:14).*' Here we are given a lot of information about who we are seeing. It is a multitude which no man could number. In the previous vision we were told nothing about how many, but it certainly wasn't a multitude. In the first vision, we were told, there were more of their kinds to be killed. The new vision tells us they are out of the Great Tribulation. We are told they are from all nations, tribes, people, and tongues. We also know they are saints, believers in Jesus Christ. How do we know? We know that they, '... *have washed their robes, and made them white in the blood of the Lamb (Revelation 7:14).*' This is a big blow for those who believe saints won't be going through the Tribulation. Some believe these are converts saved during the Tribulation. I don't think so. This is a multitude which no man could number. We can be relatively certain the Rapture is after this point in time. There couldn't be a multitude of saints which no man could number, of all nations, and kindred, and people, and tongues left on earth if the Rapture had already happened.

Let's put the number of saints into a context we can all understand. John says it's a number no man could number. Well how many can John number? John tells us the invading army is 200,000,000, (that's 200 million). If John can number 200,000,000, how many does it take to be a number he can't number?

There is one more sighting of saints in Heaven. It happens in the Book of the Revelation, Chapter 15. Here again they are those who have gotten the victory over the beast. If they have gotten victory over the beast and his mark, they had to have been in the Tribulation.

There is only one other group to make it to Heaven before Armageddon. This group is probably the biggest group to go to Heaven. This group is the Rapture group. They comprise the remaining saints alive at the end of the Tribulation and the saints who had died before the Tribulation started. The Rapture signals the end of saints on earth. Christ has come back and taken His remaining saints to Heaven, both alive and dead. We were told at the last trump the dead would be raised first and then ***we who are alive and remain*** will be changed.

This aligns with the Scriptures that call for this to happen with the last (Seventh) Trump of God. When the seventh trump begins to sound the mystery of God should be finished. What mystery is there that has not been revealed. The mystery of God is the Rapture, Watch therefore, for ye know neither the day nor the hour wherein the Son of man cometh. There is no other mystery of God. He has revealed everything else.

THE RAPTURE

The story of the Rapture is Christ coming for His people, the ripe fruit of the earth. He will take to Heaven those who have overcome the earth and maintained their testimony in Him. These will include those alive at the time and those saints who died before the Tribulation period.

The only ones left behind will be the non-believers. They will have to face 'the great winepress of the wrath of God.'

This is not the second coming of Christ. The second coming is at Armageddon and that hasn't happened yet. This event cannot be connected to the second coming, since there is no gathering of His elect from one end of Heaven to the other.

Jesus said immediately after the Tribulation there would be traumatic natural disasters. These disasters appear in The Book of the Revelation 8:5-13 through 9:1-11 and in 16:1-11. Both of these sets of 'natural disasters' end up with the Euphrates River being crossed by the invading army heading to destroy Jerusalem and then to Armageddon. God does not intend for His saints to suffer His wrath. These traumatic events occur after the Tribulation and before Armageddon.

These 'natural disasters' are discussed in more detail elsewhere in this text.

TWO TYPES OF TRIBULATION

Here is a fact I've never heard discussed before. In the Book of the Revelation we have two types of tribulation. The first type is the Great Tribulation, which applies to Christians and Jews being tortured and killed. The second period of Tribulation is the wrath of God being perpetrated on those who persecuted the saints in the Great Tribulation. Both of these times of extreme trouble on the earth are worldwide events.

The end of the Tribulation, the two witnesses being killed and the Rapture are all brought on by the Abomination of Desolation. It is the setting up of the Image (idol) of the antichrist in the Temple of God in Jerusalem. This will be the final straw. At that time the two witnesses and the saints will be raptured. They will be delivered from the wrath to come.

We have been given numerous Scriptures telling us we are not meant to receive His wrath.

Ephesians 5:6
*Let no man deceive you with vain words: for because of these things **cometh** the **wrath** of God upon the children of disobedience.*

Colossians 3:6
*For which things' sake the **wrath** of God **cometh** on the children of disobedience:*

1Thessalonians 1:10
*And to wait for his Son from heaven, whom he raised from the dead, even Jesus, which delivered us from the **wrath** to **come**.*

These Scriptures show the wrath to come is for the children of disobedience. The saints are to be delivered from this wrath.

This second Tribulation is the wrath of God brought against those who came against God's people. It will consist of great earthquakes, fire from Heaven, hail mingled with fire, a great star from Heaven burning as a lamp, etc. Some believe a nuclear bomb will be exploded in Israel. These disasters are God's wrath against those without the testimony of Jesus. These disasters will come at the end of the Great Tribulation, after the Rapture, and before Armageddon.

A SECOND TRIBULATION

In Matthew 24:29 He says, "***Immediately after the tribulation of those days*** *shall the sun be darkened, and the moon shall not give her light, and the stars shall fall from heaven, and the powers of the heavens shall be shaken:*"

Many write this off as part of the second coming of Christ. You could say that, but you have to realize it goes on for 45 days. According to Daniel, there will be a period of 45 days after the Tribulation ends before Armageddon.

Daniel is told there will be 1290 days from the time the sacrifices and oblation are stopped and the setting up of the abomination of desolation. And then he implies there will be another 45 days. These are the days Jesus said would come after the tribulation of those days, '*... the sun will be darkened, the moon shall not give her light, and the stars shall fall from heaven, and the powers of the heavens shall be shaken: (Matthew 24:29).*'

The end of the 1290 days is the end of the Great Tribulation. The 45 days after the Tribulation are for the wrath of God. The time between the 1290th day and the 1335th day is when God will show His wrath against those who came against His people. God's people will be exempted from His wrath and will be Reaped (Raptured) before this great and horrible day.

You will discover more about these events when you read the chapters devoted to the Great Tribulation and the Six Sequences.

THE SECOND COMING OF JESUS CHRIST

(Matthew 24:30-31)

And then *shall appear the sign of the Son of man in heaven: and then shall all the tribes of the earth mourn, and they shall see the Son of man coming in the clouds of heaven. And he shall send his angels with a great sound of a trumpet, and they shall gather together his elect from the four winds, from one end of heaven to the other.*

You should note these last two sections are sequential. You have the wrath of God 'immediately after the tribulation of those days'. The second coming sequence in Matthew 24:30 starts off with, 'And then'; this sets the timing of His second coming after both the Tribulation and the wrath of God. See Daniel 12:11-12 for the allocation of the time for the wrath of God after the Tribulation. We will discuss this in detail in the chapters pertaining to these events.

HOW WILL WE KNOW WHEN THE END TIMES ARE HERE

The end time can come for any of us in an instant. Once we die, we are out until the end. That will be our end time. We will not participate in anything until called by the Most High at the Rapture of the saints. We can find this in 1Thessalonians 4:15-17;

For this we say unto you by the word of the Lord, that we which are alive and remain unto the coming of the Lord shall not prevent them which are asleep. [16]For the Lord himself shall descend from heaven with a shout, with the voice of the archangel, and with the trump of God: and the dead in Christ shall rise first: [17]Then we which are alive and remain shall be caught up together with them in the clouds, to meet the Lord in the air: and so shall we ever be with the Lord.

Those saints unfortunate enough to be around at the end will know when the end is near. If you continue, you will see why I say unfortunate.

Daniel 7 tells us there will be a new empire. It will be comprised of a federation of 10 nations that will rule over the entire world. Three of the nations will be taken over by a new ruler and he will become the head of the federation comprising the One World Government.

This gives us the first clue of the end times followed by four more clues.

First Clue

There will be a One World Government initially controlled by 10 nations (Daniel 7:23).

Second Clue

Then a new ruler of the One World Government will arise and he will be brazenly anti Christian and anti Israel (Daniel 7:25).

Third Clue

Then there will be a Seven-year treaty with Israel. We are told the last week of the 70 weeks prophecy is the beginning of the end. There will be a covenant (treaty) with Israel for one week (7 years). Allegedly this treaty will be to bring peace to a trouble region (Daniel 9:24-27).

Fourth Clue

Either before, or, during this treaty the Temple will be rebuilt in Jerusalem and sacrifices will resume. We can conclude this because Daniel 9:27 says, "*he shall cause the sacrifice* (meat offering Sheep, Lamb,

Bull, Dove etc.) and the oblation (Grain Offering) *to cease*". They can't cease if they never started.

Fifth Clue

Also in Daniel 9:27, we are told halfway through the treaty, the treaty will be broken and abominations will take place until the end. In Daniel 7:25 we are told," he shall speak great words against the Most High, and shall wear out the saints of the Most High, and think to change times and laws; and they shall be given into his hand until a time, and times, and the dividing of time." I remember when my dad said he would wear me out, I didn't look forward to it, neither should the 'saints of the Most High' alive at that time. This will be the period known as the 'Great Tribulation'. It will last 1260 days (3-1/2 years). We will get into more detail about this in the chapter on the Great Tribulation.

There you have what you need to know to determine if the Great Tribulation is about to start or has started.

ARMAGEDDON

After the end of the period of God's wrath, the armies of the East are unleashed at the river Euphrates. These two Scriptures in the Book of the Revelation 9:14-16 and 16:12-16 show how Armageddon follows the period of the wrath of God.

The Euphrates is dried up so the kings of the east can get across with an army of 200,000,000. The antichrist and the false prophet use all of their minions to draw the entire world to go against Israel and God meets them at a place called Armageddon.

There are only a few places in The Book of the Revelation where Armageddon is mentioned or discussed directly. However, there are at least six areas where we have events leading up to Armageddon.

The actual event of Armageddon is found in the Book of the Revelation 16:12-16, and 19:11-21. The other references leading up to Armageddon are the Book of the Revelation 6:2-17, 9:14-21, 11:3-13 and 14:14-20.

At Armageddon, the armies of the beast are defeated by God. The antichrist and the false prophet will be taken and cast into the lake of fire where the smoke of their torment will rise forever and ever.

Satan is then taken and locked in the bottomless pit for 1000 years.

THE MILLENNIUM (1000 Year Reign with Christ)

Now comes another fact I haven't heard anyone talk about. There are still nations out there after Armageddon. They are not Christian nations, since the saints were all raptured. These nations will exist until the time of the Great White Throne Judgment at the end of the Millennium. Gog and Magog come against Jerusalem at the end of the Millennium just before the Great White Throne Judgment.

At the end of the 1000 years, Satan is let loose one more time to deceive the nations into going against God. Satan brings another battle a thousand years after Armageddon, but the result is the same. God destroys Satan's army again. Satan is then sent to his final demise in the lake of fire. That is the end of Satan and sin.

There are two more major events yet to be discussed.

THE JUDGMENT

There seems to be some question in some peoples mind about who has to appear at the Great White Throne Judgment. There are those that question whether saints will appear before the White Throne Judgment? Let's lay that to rest right now. 2Corinthians 5 says we must all appear before the judgment seat of Christ. There are more Scriptures on this, but this one removes all doubt.

So what happens at the White Throne Judgment?

First, Christ will determine if you are in the Book of Life. If you are not found in the Book of Life, '*whosoever was not found written in the book of life was cast into the lake of fire.*' This is eternal damnation. There is no redemption from the lake of fire.

Second, if Christ finds you are found in the Book of Life, then the book of works is opened and your rewards for eternity will be based on what you did with your life after salvation. Remember, what happened before you were saved was washed away by the blood of the lamb.

NEW HEAVEN AND NEW EARTH

In the Book of the Revelation Chapter 21 we are told there will be a new Heaven and a new earth. That's all we are told about the new Heaven and the new earth. There will be a new earth and there will be no sea. We aren't told where it came from or how big it is. We aren't told how we get on the new earth. However, we are told a great deal about the new Heaven. Where is heaven you might ask? Heaven is wherever God is. In The Book of the Revelation Chapter 21 it is called New Jerusalem.

Jesus told His disciples He was going to go and prepare a place for them. In the Book of the Revelation Chapter 21 we see the culmination of that promise. Yes, it comes from Heaven where Jesus had it prepared for us.

Then we get a description of the New Jerusalem coming down out of heaven.

It is illuminated by the glory of God. It is shaped in the form of a cube. It is as tall as it wide and long. It is 12,000 furlongs long, wide, and high. A furlong is 660 ft. That makes the New Jerusalem 1500 miles long, 1500 miles wide and 1500 miles high.

The walls are a hundred forty four cubits high. A standard cubit is considered to be 20 inches. That would make the wall 240 feet high.

The rest of the spectacular adornments and conditions can be read about in the Book of the Revelation 21:10-23 and 22:1-5.

REVIEW

If someone tells you the Lord could come tomorrow, you have the question. Was the Seven-year treaty signed seven years ago? He can't come until the Seven-year treaty has run its course. A look at The Book of the Revelation 14:14-21 will show you the Rapture (Reaping the ripe fruit) is connected to the wrath of God. Also; in Matthew 24:29-31, Jesus said, '[29]**Immediately after the tribulation of those days** shall the sun be darkened, and the moon shall not give her light, and the stars shall fall from heaven, and the powers of the heavens shall be shaken: [30]**And then shall appear the sign of the Son of man in heaven**: and then shall all the tribes of the earth mourn, and they shall see the Son of man coming in the clouds of heaven with power and great glory. [31]And **he shall send his angels with a great sound of a trumpet, and they shall gather together his elect from the four winds, from one end of heaven to the other.** This should make it perfectly clear. The second coming is after the Great Tribulation, and the wrath of God.

And when is the Rapture? It is at the last trump. When is the last trump? In the Book of the Revelation, there are seven trumps. The last trump is after God's two witnesses have completed their 1260 days of witnessing, have been killed, resurrected and returned to heaven. That places the seventh trump at the end of the Great Tribulation When the dead in Christ shall rise first and those alive will follow. In Chapter 14:14 of the Book of the Revelation Jesus comes in a cloud. He has a twofold mission. First is to reap the ripe fruit, the clusters of ripe fruit from the vine. The other is to reap the vine of the earth and cast it into the winepress of His wrath. We aren't told if there is a time period between the reaping of the ripe clusters and the reaping of the vine of the earth, but it will be followed by the wrath of God.

The last trump is also preceded by what appears to be a natural disaster. A great earthquake shook Jerusalem so hard a tenth of the city fell and 7000 men were killed. And we are told there is one more woe to come. This is the beginning of a series of cataclysmic events known as the wrath of God.

This would bring us to Armageddon. Armageddon is an annihilation of the armies of the antichrist and false prophet. In fact the antichrist and the false prophet are rounded up and cast alive into a lake of fire burning with brimstone. Satan is taken and locked in the bottomless pit.

This ends our little review.

Some of this information will be repeated throughout the book.

OVERVIEW OF OUR STUDY

The generally accepted end of the Great Tribulation is Armageddon. In the Book of the Revelation there are at least six separate sequences leading up to Armageddon or to events pertaining to Armageddon.

We will look at each of these sequences and then we'll look at other events that happened during this period and we will look at some of the prophecies in the Old Testament that also tell of these events

Chapter 2 BEAST AND FALSE PROPHET

THE BEAST

At the time leading up to the time of the end, a powerful group of ten nations will rise to worldwide dominance. From that group of nations, a single individual will rise to the top and will rule the world. This could be through the United Nations Security Council however; at this time no one knows for sure where they will rear their heads. The ten kings are referred to as the fourth beast or the fourth kingdom in prophecy. In the prophecy, these rulers of the fourth kingdom yield their power and authority to the one king and he will become the one we will call the antichrist. He will develop a Seven-year treaty with Israel. He will then break the treaty half way through.

Let's take a look at some of the prophecies depicting these events.

(Daniel 7:7) "*After this I saw in the night visions, and behold,* ***a fourth beast,*** *dreadful and terrible, and strong exceedingly; and it had iron teeth. It devoured, and broke in pieces, and stamped the residue with the feet of it; and it was diverse from all the beasts that were before it, and it had* ***ten horns.***"

Here, Daniel is told the fourth beast will be dreadful and terrible. Its actions will be abhorrent to the average person.

(Daniel 7:19-22) "[19]*Then I would know the truth of* ***the fourth beast,*** *which was diverse from all the others, exceeding dreadful, whose*

teeth were of iron and his nails of brass, which devoured, broke in pieces,
and stamped the residue with his feet; [20]*and of the ten horns that were in*
his head, and of the other which came up and before whom three fell, even
of the horn that had eyes and a mouth that spoke very great things, whose
look was more stout than his fellows. [21]***I beheld, and the same***
horn made war with the saints and prevailed against them
[22]*until the Ancient of Days came, and judgment was given to the saints of*
the Most High; and the time came that the saints possessed the
Kingdom".

The fourth beast will make war with the saints and will destroy them. In turn, God will destroy the fourth beast.

(Daniel 7:23-25) "[23]***The fourth beast shall be the fourth***
kingdom upon earth*, which shall be diverse from all kingdoms, and*
shall devour the whole earth*, and shall tread it down, and break it*
in pieces. [24]*And* ***the ten horns out of this kingdom are ten***
kings that shall arise*: and* ***another shall rise after them****; and*
he shall be diverse from the first, and ***he shall subdue three kings****.*
[25]*And he shall* ***speak great words against the most High****, and*
shall wear out the saints of the most High, and ***think to change***
times and laws*: and they* ***shall be given into his hand until a***
time and times and the dividing of time*.*"

The fourth beast shall rule the entire world. The antichrist will overcome three nations and then move on to be ruler over all ten nations of the beast. He will become the antichrist of prophecy and will set out to remove all followers of Christ from the face of the earth.

(Daniel 8:23-25) [23]*And in* ***the latter time*** *of their kingdom, when*
the transgressors are come to the full, a king of fierce countenance and

understanding dark sentences shall stand up. [24]*And* ***his power shall be mighty, but not by his own power,*** *and he shall destroy wondrously, and shall prosper and perform, and* ***shall destroy the mighty and the holy people.*** [25]*And through his policy also he shall cause deceit to prosper in his hand; and he shall magnify himself in his heart, and* ***by using peace shall destroy many.*** *He shall also stand up against the Prince of princes, but he shall be broken without raising a hand.*

Near the end of time as we know it, the antichrist will rise to power with the help of Satan. He will destroy both Jew and saint. He will be a deceiver and will destroy many until he is defeated by Christ.

(Daniel *9:27)* [27]*And* ***he shall confirm the covenant with many for one week:*** *and in the midst of the week he shall cause the sacrifice and the oblation to cease, and for the overspreading of abominations he shall make it desolate, even until the consummation, and that determined shall be poured upon the desolate.*

The antichrist will bring about a peace treaty between Israel and its adversaries. The treaty will be for seven years, but the antichrist will break the treaty halfway through. He will stop the sacrifices and the oblations. The demise of the antichrist will come when he sets up the abomination of desolation, the placing of his idol in the temple of God.

(Revelation 13:1-10) [1]*Then* ***I stood on the sand of the sea.*** *And I saw a beast rising up out of the sea, having seven heads and ten horns, and on his horns ten crowns, and on his heads a blasphemous name.* [2] *Now the beast which I saw was like a leopard, his feet were like the feet of a bear, and his mouth like the mouth of a lion. The* ***dragon gave him his***

power, his throne, and great authority. *3 And I saw one of his heads as if it had been mortally wounded, and* ***his deadly wound was healed****. And the entire world marveled and followed the beast. 4 So they worshiped the dragon who gave authority to the beast; and they worshiped the beast, saying, "Who is like the beast? Who is able to make war with him?" 5 And he was given a mouth speaking great things and blasphemies, and he was given authority to continue for forty-two months. 6 Then he opened his mouth in blasphemy against God, to blaspheme His name, His tabernacle, and those who dwell in heaven. 7 It was granted to him to make war with the saints and to overcome them. And authority was given him over every tribe, tongue, and nation. 8 And all that dwell upon the earth shall worship him, whose names are not written in the book of life of the Lamb slain from the foundation of the world. 9 If any man have an ear, let him hear. 10 He that leadeth into captivity shall go into captivity: he that killeth with the sword must be killed with the sword. Here is the patience and the faith of the saints.*

The beast is described and is shown to have characteristics of the previous worldwide empires. The antichrist receives his power and authority from Satan. The antichrist will be mortally wounded and then miraculously recovers. We are not told how he is wounded or when. We are only told he is mortally wounded, which means he should have died.

The rulers of the ten nations will worship Satan and draw their power from Satan. By drawing his power from Satan, the antichrist will be very powerful. He will blaspheme God and will be given power to pursue the saints for 42 months (3-1/2 years). The non-saints will worship the antichrist.

We refer to the leader of the beast as the antichrist. How do we know he is an antichrist?

> 2John 1:7 [7] *For many deceivers are entered into the world, who confess not that Jesus Christ is come in the flesh. This is a deceiver and an antichrist.*

This guy fits the description given by God for an antichrist.

We also have a specific source for the beast (antichrist) in The Book of the Revelation Chapter 11.

> (Revelation 11:7) [7] *And when they shall have finished their testimony, the beast that ascendeth out of the bottomless pit shall make war against them, and shall overcome them, and kill them.*

In this Scripture we are being told God's two witnesses will be slain by the beast from out of the bottomless pit. When Satan was cast out of heaven and onto the earth, he had the key to the bottomless pit. When he opened it, he released the beast (antichrist). The antichrist, being a demon, apparently will assume human form, probably by possessing a human of high rank, either military or political. That's only a guess. We don't have sufficient information to make an exact determination. Satan doesn't have the power to create life.

In the Book of the Revelation 13:1, John says he saw the beast rising up out of the sea. This would be the Aegean Sea. At the time John wrote the Book of the Revelation, he was a prisoner of Rome on the Island of Patmos. Patmos is part of a Greek island chain called the Dodecanese Chain. It is located on the East side of the Aegean Sea about 50 miles off the coast of Turkey, not far from Ephesus.

Some say this fourth empire, the empire of the beast will come out of the old Roman Empire. The description given in Daniel 7:19 lead me to believe it is a collection of all three previous empires. Later we'll see the 200,000,000-man army this empire will bring against Israel. This is an army as big as 2/3 of the population of the United States. This would be the army from the East (Revelation 16:12) [12]*And the sixth angel poured out his vial upon the great river Euphrates; and the water thereof was dried up, that the way of the* ***kings of the east might be prepared.***). Back in the 1950's it was said, 'China could march people six abreast into the sea and never run out of people'. How many could they put into an army today? However, this Scripture above says kings of the East; indicating more than one nation is involved. In the Book of the Revelation 9:14, we are told there are four angels loosed at the Euphrates. That would indicate four nations are involved in supplying this huge army. It's a shame we aren't given an indication of who they are.

All of the Scriptures we've looked at have enough overlap to let us know they are all talking about the same beast and the end time fourth kingdom. They paint a picture of an evil empire, speaking blasphemy about the most high and the only true God. What can we glean from these accounts?

There will be a fourth kingdom come to power on the earth at the time of the end. It will be different than any kingdom before it. It is also referred to as the fourth beast. Up till now, I had always assumed the beast was an individual. Not so, the 'beast' has ten horns which represent 10 rulers, making the beast a coalition of ten nations. This beast is described as being like a leopard, having feet like a bear and mouth like a lion. This appears to be a collection of the first three beasts or kingdoms. The best explanation I have found of this comes from J. Vernon McGee's commentary volume 5. He says the leopard would seem to be representative of the Grecian empire. The bear would represent the Medo-Persian Empire and the Mouth of a Lion would seem to represent the Babylonian Empire. If this is true, and we have a kingdom combining all three of those empires, it will be huge. That would represent just about all nations, with the exception of the Americas.

The fourth kingdom (the beast) will consist of ten kings. Out of the ten kings will come a single powerful ruler (Daniel 7:24) [24]*And* ***the ten horns out of this kingdom are ten kings that shall arise****: and* ***another shall rise after them****; and he shall be diverse from the first, and* ***he shall subdue three kings****.* He will rise to power by subduing three of the ten kings. (Daniel 7:20) [20]*and of the ten horns that were in his head, and of the other which came up and before whom three fell, even of the horn that had eyes and a mouth that spoke very great things, whose look was more stout than his fellows.* He will receive his power from the dragon (Satan) (Revelation 13:2) [2]*Now the beast which I saw was like a leopard, his feet were like the feet of a bear, and his mouth like the mouth of a lion. The* ***dragon gave him his power, his throne, and great authority.*** . He will be mortally wounded. His deadly wound will be healed (Revelation 13:3) [3] *And I saw one of his heads as if it had been mortally wounded, and* ***his deadly wound was healed****. And the entire world marveled and followed the beast.* He will negotiate a treaty with Israel to last seven years. He will then break the treaty half way through **(Daniel *9:27)*** [27]*And he shall confirm the covenant with many for one week: and in the midst of the week he shall cause the sacrifice and the oblation to cease, and for the overspreading of abominations he shall make it desolate, even until the consummation, and that determined shall be poured upon the desolate.* The remaining three and a half years will be the period of the Great

Tribulation. At the end of the Great Tribulation, the antichrist will perform an act of such abomination, so vial to God it will trigger a sequence of events that cause desolation.

The antichrist will be so bold, he will blaspheme God (Daniel 7:25) [25]*And he shall* ***speak great words against the most High****, and shall wear out the saints of the most High, and* ***think to change times and laws****: and they* ***shall be given into his hand until a time and times and the dividing of time****.*

He will make war against the holy people of God (Israel). (Daniel 8:24) [24]*And* ***his power shall be mighty, but not by his own power****; and he shall destroy wondrously, and shall prosper and perform, and* ***shall destroy the mighty and the holy people*** and then will make war with the saints. (Daniel 7:21, 25) [21]***I beheld, and the same horn made war with the saints and prevailed against them***, and [25]*And he shall* ***speak great words against the most High****, and shall wear out the saints of the most High* and will prevail against them. (Revelation 6:4)[4]*And there went out another horse that was red: and power was given to him that sat thereon to take peace from the earth, and that they should kill one another: and there was given unto him a great sword.*

He will have power over the entire earth (Daniel 7:23) [23]***The fourth beast shall be the fourth kingdom upon earth****, which shall be diverse from all kingdoms, and* ***shall devour the whole earth****, and shall tread it down, and break it in pieces.* (Revelation 13:7) [7]*And it was given unto him to make war with the saints, and to overcome them: and power was given him over* ***all kindreds, and tongues, and nations****.*

Let's just stop right here and clarify one misconception. I have been told over and over, this is all about Israel. The Tribulation is a punishment against Israel for its disobedience to God. For those that believe this, please look back at the previous quote from the Book of the Revelation 13:7. It says the antichrist will be given to make war with the **saints** and to **overcome** them. If that wasn't clear enough it goes on to say he will be given power over **all** kindred, tongues, and nations. The saints are not just anyone. They are those with the testimony of Jesus Christ. (Revelation 12:17) [17]*And the dragon was wroth with the woman, and went to make war with the remnant of her seed, which keep the commandments of God, and have the* ***testimony of Jesus Christ.*** Here we are told the antichrist finishes his attack on Israel and then goes after the saints. He is after *'the remnant of her seed'*, that *'have the testimony of Jesus Christ'*. When you talk about having the Testimony of Jesus Christ, you are talking about all of us that became a member of the family of God (remnant of her seed).

In Daniel 7:25, we see how long he will be permitted to bring his atrocities on God's people. (Daniel 7:25) [25]*...they* ***shall be given into his hand until a time and times and the dividing of time,*** (3-1/2 yrs).

The end of the antichrist will be in the lake of fire after Armageddon,

> (Revelation 19:20) [20]*And the beast was taken, and with him the false prophet that wrought miracles before him, with which he deceived them that had received the mark of the beast, and them that worshipped his image. These both were cast alive into a lake of fire burning with brimstone.*

Let's summarize what we know about the beast.

- The beast is a collection of nations with a ruthless leader (Daniel 8:23).

- This leader will blaspheme God, and he will rule the entire world (Revelation 13:6).
- This leader is referred to today as the antichrist (1John 2:18).
- The antichrist will be mortally wounded and healed by the dragon (Satan) (Revelation 13:4).
- The antichrist has the attitude of Satan and blasphemes God (Daniel 7: 25).
- He will make a Seven-year treaty with Israel and then break it half way through (Daniel 9:27).
- He along with the rest of the beast will first make war with Israel (Daniel 8: 24).
- Then, he will go after the saints of the world and will prevail against them (Daniel 7:21).
- He will be given 42 months to complete his atrocities (Revelation 13:5).
- He will be worshiped by those not in the Book of Life (Revelation 13:8).
- He will be defeated by God at Armageddon and then cast into lake of fire (Revelation 19:20).

A REVIEW OF TIMES IN PROPHECY

I need to do a refresher of the references to time in end time prophecy. We have several different references to time measurement in end time prophecy.

The most common time references are 3-1/2 years, 1260 days, 42 months, 70 weeks, and times, time & ½time (or dividing of time).

As mentioned earlier, when the Bible uses weeks as a time reference in prophecy, it is referring to years in multiples of seven. One week would represent 7 years, 70 weeks would represent seventy times 7, or 490 years. Half of a week (half of 7yrs) = 3-1/2 yrs = 42 months (@ 30 days a month) = 1260 days.

When the Bible uses the word 'time' as a time reference it means a year. 'Time' is considered to be a year. 'Times' is considered to mean two years. So, 'Times', 'time', '1/2 time' = 3-1/2 years (2 + 1 + ½ = 3-1/2)

When the angel referred to the breaking of the covenant in the middle of the week (Daniel 9:27), he was saying at 3-1/2 years into the treaty, the treaty will be broken and the Tribulation period will begin. (3-1/2years, or 42months, or 1260 days)

We have four time periods mentioned that pertain to the Tribulation period. Let's take a look at them now.

Seven years, 1260 days(42 months – 3-1/2 years) , 1290 days, and 1335 days.

Seven years is the original length of the treaty negotiated by the antichrist with Israel.

Twelve-hundred sixty days is the accepted length of the Tribulation period. This is the time the antichrist will be given to do his thing. It is the amount of time the two witnesses will have to testify to the whole world.

Twelve-hundred ninety days (Daniel 12:11) gives us another thirty days to account for. We don't have an explanation for the additional 30 days added here. It could be the sacrifices and oblations are shut down by the antichrist 30 days before the treaty is actually broken. It could be that stopping the sacrifice and oblation causes Israel to rise up and forces the antichrist to step in and break the treaty **(Daniel**

9:27) [27]*And he shall confirm the covenant with many for one week: and in the midst of the week he shall cause the sacrifice and the oblation to cease.*

Thirteen-hundred thirty-five days (Daniel 12:12) gives us another 45 days to account for. If the ending of the sacrifice and oblation is 30 days before the treaty is broken; then, we have 45 days added after the end of the Tribulation (Matthew 24:29) [29]*Immediately after the tribulation of those days shall the sun be darkened, and the moon shall not give her light, and the stars shall fall from heaven, and the powers of the heavens shall be shaken:*

This will be the time of God's wrath (Revelation 16:1) [1]*Go your ways, and pour out the bowls of the wrath of God upon the earth.*. This is the event God is going to protect us from. I believe the saints will be raptured before this time of God's wrath.

Let's look at this timeline.

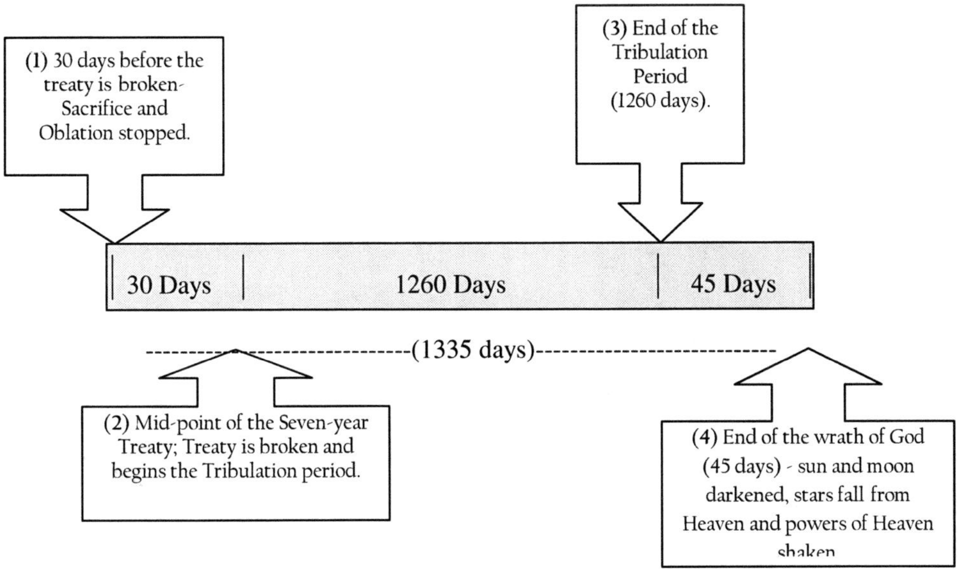
(1) 30 days before the treaty is broken- Sacrifice and Oblation stopped.
(3) End of the Tribulation Period (1260 days).
30 Days
1260 Days
45 Days
(1335 days)
(2) Mid-point of the Seven-year Treaty; Treaty is broken and begins the Tribulation period.
(4) End of the wrath of God (45 days) - sun and moon darkened, stars fall from Heaven and powers of Heaven shaken

IDENTIFYING THE BEAST (ANTICHRIST)

We are given some very specific information to help us identify the beast.

(Revelation 13:18) [18]*Here is wisdom. Let him that hath understanding count the number of the beast: for it is the number of a man; and his number is Six hundred threescore and six.*

This procedure of determining the identity of the antichrist sounds pretty simple doesn't it? When the time comes we'll just take the leaders name and add it up. If it comes out 666, we've got our man. Sorry, it isn't going to be quite that simple.

Here are some questions we need to consider when deciphering his name and number.

Is the term 'beast' referring to the coalition of nations, or the leader of the ten nations? What language are we to use to decipher the name?

The New Testament was written in Greek.

Jesus was a Jew, His language was Hebrew.

The false prophet is probably an Arab, and his language will be Aramaic, or Farsi.

The antichrist could be American or Russian or Chinese or French or Italian, or Greek.

Some of these have their own unique alphabet, making the number of the name unique to that language.

As with much of prophecy we aren't given enough information to make an informed determination at this time. At the time of the end, I believe it will be made simple. Now let's move on the antichrist's sidekick.

The Second Beast – False Prophet

In the Book of the Revelation 13:11-17 we will look at the rise of the false prophet and his powers and accomplishments.

> (Revelation 13:11) Then *I saw another beast coming up out of the earth, and he had two horns like a lamb and spoke like a dragon.*

Unlike the first beast which came up out of the Sea, this one comes 'up out of the earth'. Does this mean the second beast is home grown in Israel or, possibly comes from one of Israel's neighbors?

The two horns would normally indicate a ruler over two nations but, it doesn't say which two nations. It goes on to say he has two horns like a lamb, which could imply he is a man of peace, possibly a religious leader, such as an Imam or a Cleric of some sort. This would tie the western culture and the Muslim culture together in one kingdom (Roman Empire and the Medo-Persian Empire). He speaks like a dragon which would imply he speaks like Satan which makes him compatible with the antichrist.

> (Revelation 13:12) 12 *And he exerciseth all the power of the first beast before him, and causeth the earth and them which dwell therein to worship the first beast, whose deadly wound was healed.*

Here we see the antichrist has risen to power before the false prophet shows up on the worldwide scene. It appears this false prophet will be there to give direct support to the antichrist. He will be given the same authority as the antichrist and he gets it from the same place, the dragon (Satan). He will be a type of John the Baptist, in that he will be a religious advocate of the antichrist. He will cause the people of the earth to worship the antichrist. This false prophet will perform miracles in the presence of the antichrist and will deceive many. He too will blaspheme God. Don't be confused, he won't be blaspheming Allah. God of all heaven and earth is not the same as Allah. A Muslim would be right at home blaspheming the God of the Trinity. He will be willing to lie when the truth won't hurt. He will deceive many. Muslims believe they can lie to non-Muslims with impunity. The word of a Muslim to a non-Muslim (an infidel) means nothing.

The false prophet will draw credibility to himself by performing miracles.

> (Revelation 13:13-14) [13]*And he doeth great wonders, so that he maketh fire come down from heaven on the earth in the sight of men.* [14]*And deceiveth them that dwell on the earth by the means of those miracles which he had power to do in the sight of the beast; saying to them that dwell on the earth, that they should make an image to the beast, which had the wound by a sword, and did live.*

By performing these miracles he is able to deceive the people of the world into believing the antichrist is some sort of god. He causes the people to make an image of the antichrist. This image must be quite significant in cost because he requires '*them that dwell on the earth, that they should make an image to the beast*'. The whole world is to contribute to the building of this image. Some think this is to honor the first beast, but I think it is to initiate control and to separate the real saints from the rest of the world.

(Revelation 13:15) [15]*And he had power to give life unto the image of the beast, that the image of the beast should both speak, and cause that as many as would not worship the image of the beast* ***should be killed.***

The false prophet is able to make this image speak. We aren't told how the image speaks or what it says. The false prophet also has those that don't worship the image to be killed. Can you imagine the breadth of his power? The whole world is to worship the image of the antichrist. How do you police this? Well, that's easier than it sounds. He will have all non-Christians required to betray anyone they know that does not worship the image of the antichrist. (Micah 7:5-7) [5]*Trust ye not in a friend, put ye not confidence in a guide: keep the doors of thy mouth from her that lieth in thy bosom.* [6]*For the son dishonoureth the father, the daughter riseth up against her mother, the daughter in law against her mother in law; a man's enemies are the men of his own house.* [7]*Therefore I will look unto the LORD; I will wait for the God of my salvation: my God will hear me.* Muslims betray one another now. Any Muslim trying to convert to Christianity or any other religion is betrayed by friends or family members and they are subject to being beheaded or stoned to death. This will be the fate of practicing Christians during the time of the Tribulation.

Jesus told us in Matthew 10 we will be betrayed by family members and would be hated because of our testimony.

(Matthew 10:21-22) [21]*And the brother shall deliver up the brother to death, and the father the child: and the children shall rise up against their parents, and cause them to be put to death.* [22]*And ye shall be hated of all men for my name's sake: but he that endureth to the end shall be saved.*

This will be made easier with the introduction of the mark of the beast.

This concludes most all we know about the second beast. We only have two more references about the second beast. The first connects him to the term false prophet.

> (Revelation 16:13) [13]*And I saw three unclean spirits like frogs come out of the mouth of the dragon, and out of the mouth of the beast, and out of the mouth of the false prophet.*

Being referred to as the false prophet strengthens the belief he is a religious leader, in league with Satan and the first beast.

MARK OF THE BEAST

> (Revelation 13:16-17) [16]*And he causeth all, both small and great, rich and poor, free and bond, to receive a mark in their right hand, or in their foreheads:* [17]*And that no man might buy or sell, save he that had the mark, or the name of the beast, or the number of his name.*

If you refuse to receive the mark, you will have two problems. First the obvious, you won't be able to buy or sell. The mark of the beast sounds like a VISA Pass Card chip, or something like it, inserted under the skin. At the time the mark is instituted, it will probably seem innocent. It will be made to seem like a natural progression of the technology of the day. There will probably be all kinds of advertising to encourage everyone to participate. Later on, it will be made mandatory. We already have chips being inserted in dogs for identification. We also have had discussion of medical records chips being used in humans. You need to understand, any of these chips could be the mark of the beast. I will refuse any of these regardless of the motivation. By receiving the mark of the beast, you will be attesting to your worship of the beast. If you refuse the mark, you will not be able to buy or sell (Revelation 13:16-17) [16]*And he causeth all, both small and great, rich and poor, free and bond, to receive a mark in their right hand, or in their foreheads:* [17]*And that no man might buy or sell, save he that had the mark.* You will also be denying the deity of the antichrist and you could be put to death.

On the other hand, there are some pretty good reasons to pass on the mark of the beast and suffer those consequences.

> (Revelation 16:2) [2] *So the first went and poured out his bowl upon the earth, and a foul and loathsome sore came upon the men who had the mark of the beast and those who worshiped his image.*

> (Revelation 9:5) [5]*And to them it was given that they should not kill them, but that they should be tormented five months: and their torment was as the torment of a scorpion, when he striketh a man.*

A loathsome sore that lasts five months sounds pretty bad to me. If this isn't bad enough, God takes a position on the mark of the beast as well.

> (Revelation 14:9-11) [9] *Then a third angel followed them, saying with a loud voice, "If anyone worships the beast and his image, and receives his mark on his forehead or on his hand,* [10] *he himself shall also drink of the wine of the wrath of God, which is poured out full strength into the cup of His indignation. He shall be tormented with fire and brimstone in the presence of the holy angels and in the presence of the Lamb.* [11] *And the smoke of their torment ascends forever and ever; and they have no rest day or night, who worship the beast and his image, and whoever receives the mark of his name."*

I don't know about you, but I don't want to take a chance of falling into that category.

Now here is a group I do want to be in.

(Revelation 20:4) [4]*And I saw thrones, and they sat on them, and judgment was committed to them. Then I saw the souls of those who had been beheaded for their witness to Jesus and for the word of God, who had not worshiped the beast or his image, and had not received his mark on their foreheads or on their hands. And they lived and reigned with Christ for a thousand years.*

If you worship the beast or, receive the mark of the beast you **will not** reign with Christ.

ANTICHRIST AND FALSE PROPHET MEET THEIR END

Then the end comes to the antichrist and the false prophet.

(Revelation 19:20) [20]*'And the beast was taken, and with him the false prophet who wrought miracles in his presence, by which he deceived them that had received the mark of the beast, and them that worshiped his image. These both were cast alive into a lake of fire, burning with brimstone.'*

Here is the end of the beast and the false prophet. This also confirms the false prophet is indeed the second beast that did miracles in the presence of the first beast and the deception of the mark.

Scriptures about the ten kings and the rise of the beast and false prophet are: Daniel 7:7, 20, 24; the Book of the Revelation 12:3; 13:1; 17:3, 7, 12, 16.

Chapter 3 Fall of Satan to Earth

Preface

In this short chapter we will look at the fall of Satan to Earth and a brief look at his efforts on earth. Chapter 12 of the Book of the Revelation is a particularly interesting study because it has three separate takes on this same subject.

The Woman, the Child, and the Dragon

> (Revelation 12:1-6) [1]*Now a great sign appeared in heaven: a woman clothed with the sun, with the moon under her feet, and on her head a garland of twelve stars.* [2] *Then being with child, she cried out in labor and in pain to give birth.* [3] *And another sign appeared in heaven: behold, a great, fiery red dragon having seven heads and ten horns, and seven diadems on his heads.* [4] *His tail drew a third of the stars of heaven and threw them to the earth. And the dragon stood before the woman who was ready to give birth, to devour her Child as soon as it was born.* [5] *She bore a male Child who was to rule all nations with a rod of iron. And her Child was caught up to God and His throne.* [6] *Then the woman fled into the wilderness, where she has a place prepared by God that they should feed her there one thousand two hundred and sixty days.*

This dialog begins with a description of Israel which is also found in a dream of Joseph son of Jacob (renamed Israel by God) in Genesis 37:9.

(Genesis 37:9)[9]*And he dreamed yet another dream, and told it to his brethren and said, "Behold, I have dreamed one dream more; and behold, the sun and the moon and the eleven stars made obeisance to me."*

In verse two the woman is with child. This, of course, is a reference to the first coming of Christ.

In the Book of the Revelation 12:3-4; we see the red dragon using his tail, he '*drew a third of the stars of heaven and threw them to the earth*'. At this point there is no mention of Satan being cast out of heaven. The Scripture appears to imply Satan is sending his angels from Heaven to earth at the time of Christ's birth. Then it says Satan (the Dragon) was there waiting when Christ was born. I believe at that time he was able to move back and forth from Heaven to earth and back with complete freedom. I don't believe he is permanently kicked out of Heaven until the time of the Great Tribulation. Satan was there waiting when Christ was born but Christ was able to overcome him and He was returned to heaven.

In verse 6 we see in the last days Israel will flee from Satan to a place prepared by God. There they will be fed for 1,260 days. We can conclude they will be there for the time of the Great Tribulation.

This ends the first of the three summaries of Satan.

Satan Thrown Out of Heaven

(Revelation 12:7-9) [7]*And war broke out in heaven: Michael and his angels fought with the dragon; and the dragon and his angels fought,* [8] *but they did not prevail, nor was a place found for them in heaven any longer.* [9]*So the great dragon was cast out, that serpent of old, called the Devil and Satan, who deceives the whole world; he was cast to the earth, and his angels were cast out with him.*

In this brief summary we are told specifically that Satan and his angels are kicked out of Heaven by the angel Michael. We are also told of Satan's greatest asset, deception. He will '*deceive the whole world.*' He is the great deceiver.

(Revelation 12:10) [10]*Then I heard a loud voice saying in heaven, "Now salvation, and strength, and the kingdom of our God, and the power of His Christ have come, for the accuser of our brethren, who accused them before our God day and night, has been cast down.*

This is confirmation of Satan being cast down to earth. This is Satan unleashed on the earth as he was unleashed against Job.

(Revelation 12:11) [11]*And they overcame him by the blood of the Lamb and by the word of their testimony, and they did not love their lives to the death.*

This I believe gives us the timing of Satan's getting booted out of Heaven. This appears to refer to the killing of the saints during the Tribulation period. The saints are sticking to their testimony of Jesus Christ and they are willing to die for their faith in Jesus. The saints of the Great Tribulation will refuse to worship the beast or his image and for that they will be killed.

(Revelation 12:12) [12]*Therefore rejoice, O heavens, and you who dwell in them! Woe to the inhabitants of the earth and the sea! For the devil has come down to you, having great wrath, because he knows that he has a short time."*

This is a reaffirmation of the Woe, or dreadful time that is to come as the result of Satan being cast out of Heaven to the earth. It says here he has but a short time. This adds to the confirmation of when Satan is cast out of Heaven. It says *because he knows that he has a short time.*

We are not told how much time. Was he cast out of Heaven before or after the rise of the beast? In the Book of the Revelation Chapter 9 we are told a star fell from Heaven with the key to the bottomless pit. Is this when Satan was cast out of Heaven? We are told in Chapter 11: 7, of the Book of the Revelation, that the antichrist is loosed from the bottomless pit. The antichrist had to have been released onto the earth before the making of the Seven-year treaty, since Daniel 9:27 says the antichrist will be the one to confirm the covenant with many for one week.

The Woman Persecuted

> (Revelation 12:13-16) [13] *Now when the dragon saw that he had been cast to the earth, he persecuted the woman who gave birth to the male Child.* [14] *But the woman was given two wings of a great eagle, that she might fly into the wilderness to her place, where she is nourished for a time and times and half a time, from the presence of the serpent.* [15] *So the serpent spewed water out of his mouth like a flood after the woman, that he might cause her to be carried away by the flood.* [16] *But the earth helped the woman, and the earth opened its mouth and swallowed up the flood which the dragon had spewed out of his mouth.*

When Satan is permanently cast out of Heaven and to the earth, he will go after Israel. We know this because it says, 'he persecuted the woman who gave birth to the male Child'. The male child, of course is the savior of the world, Jesus Christ. The woman, therefore, refers to Israel. During the Tribulation, Israel will flee from the attack of the Beast with help from the earth (other countries of the world). Israel will be on the run for 1260 days.

> (Revelation 12:17) [17]*And the dragon was wroth with the woman, and went to make war with the remnant of her seed, which keep the commandments of God, and have the testimony of Jesus Christ.*

When the Beast is unable to capture all of the Israelites because of help from other nations, he will go after the rest of the saints in these other nations.

> (Revelation 13:7) [7]'*It was granted to him to make war with the saints and to overcome them. And authority was given him over every tribe, tongue, and nation.*'

This tells us, at some point during the Tribulation, the thrust of Satan's attacks will be directed toward the rest of the world, not just Israel. Remember Satan is controlling the beast (antichrist). They are not one in the same. The antichrist is given power and authority over '*every tribe, tongue, and nation*'.

Satan's Plan

When Satan is cast out of Heaven, never to return, he devises a plan to wipe out God's people. He creates the Beast with a massive army and enormous power to do his bidding.

In the following verses, I believe we see the initial creation of the Beast (antichrist) and his army.

> (Revelation 9:1-11) [1]*And the fifth angel sounded, and I saw a star fall from heaven unto the earth: and to him was given the key of the bottomless pit.* [2]*And he opened the bottomless pit; and there arose a*

smoke out of the pit, as the smoke of a great furnace; and the sun and the
air were darkened by reason of the smoke of the pit. [3]*And there came out*
of the smoke locusts upon the earth: and unto them was given power, as
the scorpions of the earth have power. [4]*And it was commanded them that*
they should not hurt the grass of the earth, neither any green thing,
neither any tree; but only those men which have not the seal of God in
their foreheads. [5]*And to them it was given that they should not kill them,*
but that they should be tormented five months: and their torment was as
the torment of a scorpion, when he striketh a man. [6]*And in those days*
shall men seek death, and shall not find it; and shall desire to die, and
death shall flee from them. [7]*And the shapes of the locusts were like unto*
horses prepared unto battle; and on their heads were as it were crowns
like gold, and their faces were as the faces of men.[8]*And they had hair as*
the hair of women, and their teeth were as the teeth of lions.[9]*And they had*
breastplates, as it were breastplates of iron; and the sound of their wings
was as the sound of chariots of many horses running to battle.[10]*And they*
had tails like unto scorpions, and there were stings in their tails: and
their power was to hurt men five months. [11]*And they had a king over them,*
which is the angel of the bottomless pit, whose name in the Hebrew tongue
is Abaddon, but in the Greek tongue hath his name Apollyon.

This appears to be Satan reaching down into the bottomless pit and drawing back out his beasts of old and forming a new more powerful empire than has ever been seen on earth before. He creates the fourth beast of the earth. We get an acknowledgement of this in the Book of the Revelation Chapter 11.

(Revelation 11:7) [7]*And when they shall have finished their testimony, the beast that ascendeth out of the bottomless pit shall make war against them, and shall overcome them, and kill them.*

Here, we are told the beast (antichrist) is indeed pulled up out of the bottomless pit. He would then be properly classified as one of Satan's demons. He shows his contempt for God by killing his two witnesses.

This concludes our study of Satan being cast to earth. For additional studies in this area see the chapter on the Beast and the False Prophet.

Chapter 4 Saints in Heaven

Preface

Of all the issues before us about saints in Heaven and who gets there and when, there is only one criterion that matters. Is your name in the Lamb's Book of Life? If you have not accepted Jesus Christ as your savior, your redeemer, you are not going to Heaven. If you are in the Book of Life, do you have works to justify your faith? If not, you may be in danger of being removed from the Book of Life. I know this is hard to hear but, I didn't say it, Jesus did.

We will cover these topics and more in this chapter.

ABSENT FROM THE BODY, PRESENT WITH THE LORD

All my life I've been told, if we are in the Lambs Book of Life at the time we die, we go immediately to Heaven. Paul is credited with saying, 'absent from the body, present with the Lord'. I've said it many times. Let's take a look at what he really said.

> (2Corinthians 5: 6-10) [6]*Therefore we are always confident, knowing that, whilst we are at home in the body, we are absent from the Lord;* [7]*for we walk by faith, not by sight.* [8]*We are confident, I say, and willing rather to be absent from the body and to be present with the Lord.* [9]*Therefore we labor, that, whether present or absent, we may be accepted by Him.* [10]*For we must all appear before the judgment seat of Christ, that every one may receive the things done in his body, according to what he hath done, whether it be good or bad.*

A closer examination of these verses shows Paul is pointing out we can't be in two places at once. If we are here, we can't be there and vice versa. He does not say we go from death directly to Heaven. He does say we must go to the judgment seat of Christ. If you are born again and died today, the next thing you would know is the Rapture. The Scripture says we sleep until the time of the Rapture.

> (1Thessalonians 4: 13-16) [13]*But I would not have you to be ignorant, brethren, concerning them which are asleep, that ye sorrow not, even as others which have no hope.* [14]*For if we believe that Jesus died and rose again, even so them also which sleep in Jesus will God bring with him.* [15]*For this we say unto you by the word of the Lord, that we which are alive and remain unto the coming of the Lord shall not prevent them which are asleep.* [16]*For the Lord himself shall descend from heaven with a shout, with the voice of the archangel, and with the trump of God: and the dead in Christ shall rise first:*

I have one final point on absent from the body, present with the Lord. If we go straight to Heaven when we die, who gets raptured? Who are the dead that go first?

Let's look at a couple of examples in the Bible of people dying and what happens to them.

BEGGAR AND THE RICH MAN

The Bible gives us examples showing we do not go directly from the death to Heaven.

In the Book of Luke we have an account of a beggar named Lazarus and an anonymous rich man.

(Luke 16:19-31) [19] *There was a certain rich man, who was clothed in purple and fine linen and fared sumptuously every day. [20]And there was a certain beggar named Lazarus, who was laid at his gate, full of sores. [21]and desiring to be fed with the crumbs which fell from the rich man's table. Moreover the dogs came and licked his sores. [22]And it came to pass that the beggar died, and was carried by the angels into Abraham's bosom. The rich man also died, and was buried. [23]And in hell, being in torment, he lifted up his eyes and saw Abraham afar off and Lazarus in his bosom. [24]And he cried and said, `Father Abraham, have mercy on me, and send Lazarus that he may dip the tip of his finger in water and cool my tongue; for I am tormented in this flame.' [25]But Abraham said, `Son, remember that thou in thy lifetime received thy good things, and likewise Lazarus evil things; but now he is comforted and thou art tormented. [26]And besides all this, between us and you there is a great gulf fixed, so that they who would pass from here to you cannot; neither can they pass to us, that would come from there.' [27]Then he said, `I pray thee therefore, father, that thou wouldest send him to my father's house, [28]for I have five brethren, that he may testify unto them lest they also come into this place of torment.' [29]Abraham said unto him, `They have Moses and the prophets; let them hear them.' [30]And he said, `Nay, father Abraham; but if one went unto them from the dead, they will repent.' [31]And Abraham said unto him, `if they hear not Moses and the prophets, neither will they be persuaded though one rose from the dead.'*

This account shows these two men went to different places after death. Neither went to Heaven. The rich man went to hell and Lazarus went to Abraham's bosom. Neither is in Heaven. Neither is in the presence of the Lord.

What are these two places? Are they permanent places, or are they temporary holding places? I believe the answer, in part, can be found in the Book of the Revelation 20:11-15.

> (Revelation *20:11-15)* [11]*And I saw a great white throne, and him that sat on it, from whose face the earth and the heaven fled away; and there was found no place for them.* [12]*And I saw the dead, small and great, stand before God; and the books were opened: and another book was opened, which is the book of life: and the dead were judged out of those things which were written in the books, according to their works.* [13]*And the sea gave up the dead which were in it; and death and hell delivered up the dead which were in them: and they were judged every man according to their works.* [14]*And death and hell were cast into the lake of fire. This is the second death.* [15]*And whosoever was not found written in the book of life was cast into the lake of fire.*

From this we can glean there are holding places for the souls of those that die, whether saint or sinner.

Now we will look at another biblical example of what happens after death.

JESUS AND THE THIEF ON THE CROSS

This example of an after death destination is one of the most abused Scriptures in the Bible. This is the account of the discourse between Christ on the cross and the thief on the cross.

In Luke 23:43 Jesus told the thief on the cross, '*I tell you the truth, today you will be with me in Paradise.*

That sounds pretty simple doesn't it? It sounds like they will be in Heaven together that same day. There is one little problem. Jesus didn't go to Heaven that day. In fact, Jesus didn't go to Heaven until the third day. I'm not saying they weren't together in Paradise that same day but, they weren't in Heaven.

(John 20: 1) [1]The first day of the week cometh Mary Magdalene early, when it was yet dark, unto the sepulchre, and seeth the stone taken away from the sepulchre.

This is on the first day of the week after the crucifixion, the third day after Jesus told the thief on the cross that he would be with Him in Paradise.

*(John 20:15-17) [15]Jesus saith unto her, Woman, why weepest thou? Whom seekest thou? She, supposing him to be the gardener, saith unto him, Sir, if thou have borne him hence, tell me where thou hast laid him, and I will take him away. [16]Jesus saith unto her, Mary. She turned herself, and saith unto him, Rabboni; which is to say, Master. [17]Jesus saith unto her, '**Touch me not; for I am not yet ascended to my Father**: but go to my brethren, and say unto them, I ascend unto my Father, and your Father; and to my God, and your God.'*

On the third day, Jesus told Mary 'He has not ascended to his Father'. He had not received His purified body. If He had not ascended to His Father, where did He go upon His physical death? Obviously, He didn't go to Heaven.

We do have an indication Jesus went down into hell first.

(Ephesians *4:9-10) [9]Now that he ascended, what is it but that he also descended first into the lower parts of the earth? [10]He that descended is the same also that ascended up far above all heavens, that he might fill all things.*

He descended into the lower parts of the earth (hell, bottomless pit?). This was Christ overcoming the sins of man; He had taken upon Himself, a provision that allows for the remission of our sins. If He hadn't overcome them, how could He remit them?

(Acts 2:31) [31]*He seeing this before spake of the resurrection of Christ, that his soul was* ***not left in hell****, neither his flesh did see corruption.*

He wasn't in hell very long. Where did He go after that? He ascended after He descended. He didn't go to the Father until after the third day. Apparently, He spent less than a day in the lower parts of the earth, since He had an appointment to meet the thief from the cross in Paradise that same day and we know Jesus does not and cannot lie. Well what happened you ask? First we need to take a look at Paradise. Where is it? What is it?

PARADISE

If Jesus didn't go to Heaven, then where is Paradise? We know Jesus cannot lie, so we know He went to Paradise as He promised the thief. So where is Paradise?

We have two more accounts in the Bible where Paradise is mentioned: 2Corinthians Chapter 12 and the Book of the Revelation Chapter 2.

In 2Corinthians Chapter 12, Paul is discussing his encounter with Jesus (or the Holy Spirit) on the road to Damascus, where he started his miraculous conversion to Christianity.

(2Corinthians 12:2-4) '[2]*I knew a man in Christ above fourteen years ago, (whether in the body, I cannot tell; or whether out of the body, I cannot tell: God knoweth;) such an one caught up to the* <u>*third heaven*</u>*.* [3]*And I knew such a man, (whether in the body, or out of the body, I cannot tell: God knoweth;)* [4]*How that he was caught up into* <u>*paradise*</u>*, and heard unspeakable words, which it is not lawful for a man to utter.'*

Paul tells us here in verse 2 a man was caught up to the third heaven and in verse 4 he was caught up to Paradise. It appears he is saying they are the same place. But, where are they? Do they only exist in the spiritual realm?

Now we will look at the only other reference to Paradise in the Bible. It is located in the Book of the Revelation Chapter 2,

(Revelation *2:7)* [7]*'He that hath an ear, let him hear what the Spirit saith unto the churches; To him that overcometh will I give to eat of the tree of life, which is in the midst of the paradise of God'.*

Now we are getting somewhere. We are told Paradise is where the tree of life is. So, does the Bible tell us where the tree of life is? Yes. If you will recall, during the creation God created the Garden of Eden on the earth.

(Genesis 2:8-9) [8]*And the LORD God planted a garden eastward in Eden; and there he put the man whom he had formed.* [9]*And out of the ground made the LORD God to grow every tree that is pleasant to the sight, and good for food;* <u>*the tree of life*</u> *also in the midst of the garden, and the* <u>*tree of knowledge*</u> *of good and evil.*

You should also remember Adam and Eve ate of the Tree of Knowledge of Good and Evil. Do you remember the reason they were kicked out of the Garden? They were not kicked out because they ate of the tree of knowledge. They were kicked out to prevent them from eating of the Tree of life. We are told in Genesis 3, the Garden became a forbidden place when he expelled Adam and Eve for eating from the tree of knowledge of good and evil and to prevent them from eating of the Tree of Life and living forever.

(Genesis 3:22-24) 22'*And the LORD God said, Behold, the man is become as one of us, to know good and evil: and now, lest he put forth his hand, and take also of the tree of life, and eat, and live for ever:* 23*Therefore the LORD God sent him forth from the garden of Eden, to till the ground from whence he was taken.* 24*So he drove out the man; and he placed at the east of the garden of Eden Cherubims, and a flaming sword which turned every way, to keep the way of the tree of life'*

We are not given any indication the Garden of Eden was removed from the earth. It was merely blocked from human access. We have no other proof of where Paradise is. We have no tangible proof it is being used as a holding place for the spirits of the saints until the judgment. But we don't have any proof it isn't. We do have an account of where the Tree of Life will be and may be now.

(Revelation 22:2) 2*In the midst of the street of it, and on either side of the river, was there the tree of life, which bare twelve manner of fruits, and yielded her fruit every month: and the leaves of the tree were for the healing of the nations.*

This is from the discourse describing the New Jerusalem as the place where the Tree of Life will be. At that time the New Jerusalem will be on earth.

Will the Tree of Life come back with the New Jerusalem or, is it still here in the Garden of Eden and the New Jerusalem will be placed there?

One more limiting factor on the location of Paradise, according to the beggar and the rich man account, you can see hell from Paradise, so they are in relatively close proximity to one another. Jesus said Paradise exists. Obviously, the Garden of Eden is a Paradise created by God. Is it the Paradise spoken of by Christ on the cross? We'll have to wait for His return or our own death to find out.

CAN WE GO TO HEAVEN WITHOUT DYING

Yes, it is possible to go to Heaven without dying first. We have a couple of accounts of this happening. There are two that stand out in my mind; Enoch, who walked with God and Elijah, who was taken up in a whirlwind.

> (Genesis 5:24) '*and Enoch walked with God: and he was not; for God took him.*'

Apparently God was so taken with Enoch (the father of Methuselah) He couldn't wait to get him to Heaven. So, God just took him.

The other one was Elijah, (2Kings 2:11) '*....and Elijah went up by a whirlwind into heaven.*'

Neither of these experienced a physical death. We know these two went to Heaven. We are sure Moses went to Heaven but it was after he died. Moses appeared with Elias (Elijah) on the Mount of Transfiguration. They met with a transfigured Jesus.

> (Mark 9: 2-4) [2]*And after six days Jesus taketh with him Peter, and James, and John, and leadeth them up into an high mountain apart by themselves: and he was transfigured before them.* [3]*And his raiment became shining, exceeding white as snow; so as no fuller on earth can*

white them. [4]And there appeared unto them Elias with Moses: and they were talking with Jesus.

They are probably included in with the 24 elders in John's account in the Book of the Revelation Chapter 4.

These are the only two accounts of saints taken to Heaven and bypassing death.

ELDERS IN HEAVEN

In the Book of the Revelation, we do have actual accounts of saints in Heaven. However, we are not given any names. We do know three names from the Scriptures we just looked at. However, we have accounts of 24 Elders. Who are the other twenty-one? We don't know.

When John was taken to Heaven, he gave an account of what he saw there. In the Book of the Revelation Chapter 4, John is taken in the spirit to Heaven and to the throne room of God. He goes to some detail to describe the beings and surroundings he saw there. The only reference he made to human saints in Heaven upon his arrival was in verse 4,

(Revelation 4:4) [4]*And round about the throne were four and twenty seats: and upon the seats I saw four and twenty elders sitting, clothed in white raiment; and they had on their heads crowns of gold.'*

There is no mention of who they are. We know three of them: Enoch, Elijah, and Moses. You could put together a list of prospective elders. My list would include Noah, Abraham, King David, Jacob (renamed Israel), Joshua, Joseph, Caleb, Job, Isaiah, Daniel, 11

Disciples, and of course Paul. Most would probably want John the Baptist in there. I considered him, but according to Jesus, he is already on the list. In Matthew 11:14, Jesus was being questioned by the disciples about John the Baptist and he explains John the Baptist was in fact Elias (Elijah).

(Matthew 11:*14*) [14]'*And if ye will receive it, this is Elias, which was for to come.*'

This was also prophesied in Malachi Chapter 3.

(Malachi 3: 1-5) [1]*Behold, I will send my messenger, and he shall prepare the way before me: and the LORD, whom ye seek, shall suddenly come to his temple, even the messenger of the covenant, whom ye delight in: behold, he shall come, saith the LORD of hosts.*' and in Malachi 4:[5]*Behold, I will send you Elijah the prophet before the coming of the great and dreadful day of the LORD.*

Does this imply Elijah is both John the Baptist and one of the Witnesses during the Tribulation?

That was a long way around to say we don't know who the twenty-one elders will be.

SAINTS FROM THE TRIBULATION IN HEAVEN

When John gave his first description of whom and what he saw in Heaven, the only saints were the twenty-four elders. He doesn't mention any other saints in Heaven again until the Book of the Revelation Chapter 6.

(Revelation 6:9-11) [9]*When He opened the fifth seal, I saw under the altar the souls of those who had been slain for the word of God and for the testimony which they held.* [10] *And they cried with a loud voice, saying, "How long, O Lord, holy and true, until you judge and avenge our blood on those who dwell on the earth?"* [11] *Then a white robe was given to each of them; and it was said to them that they should rest a little while longer, until both the number of their fellow servants and their brethren, who would be killed as they were, was completed.*

These verses are after the fifth seal has been opened. At that point in time the Tribulation has been going on for some time. There is only one more seal before Armageddon. A fourth of the earth is being killed with the sword, hunger, death and the beasts of the earth.

(Revelation 6:8) [8]*And I looked, and behold a pale horse: and his name that sat on him was Death, and Hell followed with him. And power was given unto them over the fourth part of the earth, to kill with sword, and with hunger, and with death, and with the beasts of the earth.*

We see these souls were slain for their testimony, given white robes, and are before the throne under the altar. If they had been there when John arrived, he would have seen them and mentioned them. They are to wait until '*the number of their fellow servants and their brethren, who would be killed as they were, should be fulfilled*' (Revelation 6:11) (1/4th of mankind). They are to wait until the rest of them are killed as they were killed. In other words, they were killed in the Great Tribulation.

In the Book of the Revelation Chapter 7, John gives us a better account of who these saints are, and where they came from.

(Revelation 7:9) [9]"*After this I beheld, and, lo, a great multitude, which no man could number, of all nations, and kindreds, and people, and tongues, stood before the throne, and before the Lamb, clothed with white robes, and palms in their hands;"*

John sees '*A great multitude which no man could number*'. If these had been there, before the throne, when John was there in Chapter 4, I'm sure he would have mentioned them. So, if they weren't there before, when did they get there? Fortunately John tells us.

> (Revelation 7:13-17) [13]*And one of the elders answered, saying unto me, What are these which are arrayed in white robes? and whence came they?* [14]*And I said unto him, Sir, thou knowest. And he said to me, These are they which came out of great tribulation, and have washed their robes, and made them white in the blood of the Lamb.* [15]*Therefore are they before the throne of God, and serve him day and night in his temple: and he that sitteth on the throne shall dwell among them.* [16]*They shall hunger no more neither thirst any more; neither shall the sun light on them, nor any heat.* [17]*For the Lamb which is in the midst of the throne shall feed them, and shall lead them unto living fountains of waters: and God shall wipe away all tears from their eyes.*

These are saints who died in the Great Tribulation and did not worship the beast or receive the mark. These were slain for their testimony and they overcame the beast. They did not take the easy way out. They stood fast to their faith in Jesus Christ. These include the saints mentioned in the Book of the Revelation 6:9-11. The number of them has increased from 'he saw souls' to 'a great multitude, which no man could number'. Also note they are from all nations, and kindred, and people, and tongues. They are saints from all over the world, not just Israel.

I believe these that die during the Tribulation have a special blessing from God.

> (Revelation 14:13) [13]"*.....blessed are the dead, which die in the Lord from henceforth. Yea, saith the Spirit, that they may rest from their labours: and their works do follow them.*"

I believe this refers to all the saints who die during the Tribulation. This blessing is they don't go to the grave. They go from death to Heaven and are forever in the presence of the Lord, in addition to getting to rule and reign with Christ during the Millennium.

THE RAPTURE

What about the saints that died before the Great Tribulation? They don't go to Heaven until the end of the Tribulation.

> (1Corinthians 15:52) [52]*In a moment, in the twinkling of an eye, at the last trump: for the trumpet shall sound, and the dead shall be raised incorruptible, and we shall be changed.*

I believe the last trump is the seventh trump in the Book of the Revelation Chapter 11.

> (Revelation 11:15) [15]*And the seventh angel sounded; and there were great voices in heaven, saying, The kingdoms of this world are become the kingdoms of our Lord, and of his Christ; and he shall reign for ever and ever.*

First, let's verify that the last trump referred to in 1Corinthians 15:22 is the last trump of the Book of the Revelation.

(Revelation 10:7) [7]*But in the days of the voice of the seventh angel, when he shall begin to sound, the mystery of God should be finished, as he hath declared to his servants the prophets.*

What is the mystery of God spoken of here? As far as I know, the only mystery of God is the Rapture. God has revealed everything else.

(Matthew 24:36)[36]*But of that day and hour knoweth no man, no, not the angels of heaven, but my Father only.*

So, when the seventh trump begins to sound, the mystery of God, the Rapture, will be finished.

I have a couple of points to make about the timing of the Rapture.

During the Tribulation there was 'a *great multitude, which no man could number, of all nations, and kindreds, and people, and tongues*' of saints saved out of the Tribulation. If there was a Rapture of the saints prior to the Tribulation, where did this multitude which no man could number come from?

In the Book of the Revelation Chapter 13 the antichrist was granted to make war with the saints and to overcome them. If the saints were raptured before the Tribulation, why was the antichrist granted to make war with the saints that weren't there?

(Revelation 13:7) [7]*It was granted to him to make war with the saints and to overcome them. And authority was given him over every tribe, tongue, and nation.*

SAINTS IN HEAVEN'S ARMY TO ARMAGEDDON

The next move of the saints will be as a part of the army of Heaven that follows Jesus to Armageddon.

(Revelation 19:14) [14]*And the armies which were in heaven followed him upon white horses, clothed in fine linen, white and clean.*

The armies of the world are defeated and the antichrist and false prophet are cast into the lake of fire.

(Revelation 19:20) [20]*And the beast was taken, and with him the false prophet that wrought miracles before him, with which he deceived them that had received the mark of the beast, and them that worshipped his image. These both were cast alive into a lake of fire burning with brimstone.*

THE MILLENNIUM

After Armageddon the saints in the armies of Heaven do not return to heaven. They are to reign with Christ on earth for a thousand years.

(Revelation 20:4) [4]*And I saw thrones, and they sat upon them, and judgment was given unto them: and I saw the souls of them that were beheaded for the witness of Jesus, and for the word of God, and which had not worshipped the beast, neither his image, neither had received his mark upon their foreheads, or in their hands; and they lived and reigned with Christ a thousand years.*

During the Millennium there will still be nations around the world. They will not be Christian nations. These are the nations to be ruled and reigned by the saints.

(Revelation 20:6) [6]*Blessed and holy is he that hath part in the first resurrection* (Rapture): *on such the second death hath no power, but they shall be priests of God and of Christ, and shall reign with him a thousand years.*

(Revelation 11:15) [15]*And the seventh angel sounded; and there were great voices in heaven, saying, The kingdoms of this world are become the kingdoms of our Lord, and of his Christ; and he shall reign for ever and ever.*

(Revelation 5:10) [10]*And hast made us unto our God kings and priests: and we shall reign on the earth.*

The saints are made to be kings and priests to rule and reign. We are told these same saints will reign on earth with Christ for a thousand years.

We won't discuss it here, but Satan will be incarcerated in the bottomless pit during the Millennium and released just before the judgment to weave his evil web to tempt the nations to come against God one more time, only to be defeated again.

WHITE THRONE JUDGMENT

At the end of the thousand years, the saints and sinners will face the White Throne Judgment.

(Revelation 20:12) [12]*And I saw the dead, small and great, stand before God; and the books were opened: and another book was opened, which is the book of life: and the dead were judged out of those things which were written in the books, according to their works.*

This is an account of the dead being called to the Great White Throne Judgment. They are called from the sea, death, and hell. I don't have an explanation of why the sea was called out separately. However, they all three contain the unrighteous. The dead in Christ will have been resurrected at the time of the Rapture, leaving only non-believers on the earth or in the sea, death, and hell.

Some people claim the Saints will not be judged at the Great White Throne Judgment, but at the Judgment Seat of Christ, the so-called BEMA seat. I disagree. I cannot find a single reference to this happening. I believe the Bema Seat of Christ and the White Throne Judgment are the same. According to Paul in 2Corinthians Chapter 5 we all must face judgment. Nowhere does it say saints to the Judgment Seat of Christ and all others to the White Throne Judgment.

> (2Corinthians 5:10) [10]*For we must all appear before the judgment seat of Christ; that every one may receive the things done in his body, according to that he hath done, whether it be good or bad.*

Why are the saints to appear before the judgment? It is to verify for all, they are in the Book of Life. Then their works since salvation will be evaluated.

> (Revelation 20:12) [12]*'and the dead were judged out of those things which were written in the books, according to their works.'*

How many times have we been told salvation is not of works, but of faith in Jesus Christ? Can we get to eternity without works?

> (Ephesians 2:8) [8]*For by grace are ye saved through faith; and that not of yourselves: it is the gift of God:* [9]*Not of works, lest any man should boast.*

> *(Galatians 2:16)* [16]*Knowing that a man is not justified by the works of the law, but by the faith of Jesus Christ, even we have believed in Jesus*

Christ, that we might be justified by the faith of Christ, and not by the works of the law: for by the works of the law shall no flesh be justified.

(2Timothy 3:15) [15]*And that from a child thou hast known the holy scriptures, which are able to make thee wise unto salvation through faith which is in Christ Jesus.*

Now let's look at a side of works that no one seems to want to pay attention to. What if we have no works? What if our sole involvement after salvation is to be a pew warmer?

Jesus taught on this in the parable of the sower. (Matthew 13:18) [18]"*Hear ye therefore the parable of the sower.*"

Hearer #1

(Matthew 13:19) [19]*When any one heareth the word of the kingdom, and understandeth it not, then cometh the wicked one, and catcheth away that which was sown in his heart. This is he which received seed by the way side.*

The seed never took hold, Hearer only.

Hearer #2

(Matthew 13:20-21) [20]*But he that received the seed into stony places, the same is he that heareth the word, and anon with joy receiveth it;* [21]*Yet hath he not root in himself, but dureth for a while: for when tribulation or persecution ariseth because of the word, by and by he is offended*

Received the Word but never acted on it, eventually, lost his way.

Hearer #3

(Matthew 13:22) [22]*He also that received seed among the thorns is he that heareth the word; and the care of this world, and the deceitfulness of riches, choke the word, and he becometh unfruitful.*

Basically the same as hearer #2, believed but eventually lost his way.

Hearer #4

Matthew 13:23) [23]*But he that received seed into the good ground is he that heareth the word, and understandeth it; which also beareth fruit, and bringeth forth, some an hundredfold, some sixty, some thirty.*

This parable is about the fruit each of us produces. We produce fruit by works in some sort of ministry. It doesn't have to be ministry in the church, but it does have to work toward the furthering of the gospel of Jesus Christ. Jesus knows and sees all. He is the only one that needs to know what you are doing to further His gospel. He needs to be able to see you are bearing fruit through good works, and believe me he sees all, including your heart.

By my reckoning, Hearers one, two, and three won't make it past the White Throne Judgment. Two and three appear to have been saved in the beginning, but their faith wasn't cultivated and eventually it died.

Which hearer are you? I hope you're not hearer one, two, or three. God says they don't bear fruit. What do you do when your plant doesn't bear fruit? You cut it down and cast it into the fire. James tells us more about faith and works.

There are some that think once saved always saved. I suggest they read and take the following verses to heart.

(Revelation 3:15-16) [15]*I know thy works, that thou art neither cold nor hot: I would thou wert cold or hot.* [16]*So then because thou art lukewarm, and neither cold nor hot, I will spue thee out of my mouth.*

(James 2:17) [17]*Even so faith, if it hath not works, is dead, being alone,*

(James 2:26) [26]*For as the body without the spirit is dead, so faith without works is dead also.*

James tells us faith may not be enough to have your name kept in the Book of Life. When you accepted Christ as your savior, your name was entered into the Book of Life. We have seen from James and Jesus, it can be removed.

If you are not in the Book of Life, your works will not matter.

(Revelation 20:15) [15]*And whosoever was not found written in the book of life was cast into the lake of fire.*

If you are in the Book of Life, your rewards will be based on your works.

(Matthew 6:27) [27]*For the Son of man shall come in the glory of his Father with his angels; and then he shall reward every man according to his works.*

Some would interpret this as every person will be rewarded based on their works. There is one big problem with that idea. At the judgment, those not found in the Book of Life will be cast into the lake of fire. It will probably be pretty difficult to receive your rewards for good deeds if you are in the lake of fire.

(Revelation *20:15)* [15]*And whosoever was not found written in the book of life was cast into the lake of fire.*

I need to summarize works.

Works alone cannot get you into the Book of Life. Faith gets you into the Book of Life. Faith over time without works dies. When faith dies or becomes lukewarm, you can be removed from the Book of Life. This is based on Scripture not feelings. Now let's look back to the beggar and the rich man.

(Revelation 20:13) [13]*And the sea gave up the dead which were in it; and death and hell delivered up the dead which were in them.*

To me, this is saying, no matter where you are in death, you will be called to the judgment. Death and hell gave up their dead to appear at the judgment. After the judgment the rich man does **not** go back to hell. He and all others not found in the Book of Life will be cast into the lake of fire.

(Revelation 20:15) [15]*And whosoever was not found written in the book of life was cast into the lake of fire.*

Since the beggar wasn't sent to hell before the judgment, we have to believe he was a saint (a believer in Christ). As a saint he would have taken part in the Rapture.

(1Corinthians 15:52) [52]*In a moment, in the twinkling of an eye, at the last trump: for the trumpet shall sound, and the dead shall be raised incorruptible, and we shall be changed.*

At the Great White Throne Judgment your name will be looked up in the Book of Life. If it is found there, you will then be looked up in the book of works. Your rewards will be announced and then you will proceed to eternity with God and Christ.

The true saints will not face the threat of the lake of fire.

(Revelation 20:5-6) [5]*But the rest of the dead lived not again until the thousand years were finished. This is the first resurrection.* [6]*Blessed and holy is he that hath part in the first resurrection (Rapture): on such the second death hath no power, but they shall be priests of God and of Christ, and shall reign with him a thousand years.*

The saints will be there to receive notice of their rewards for eternity, based on their works.

(Revelation 20:12) [12]*And I saw the dead, small and great, stand before God; and the books were opened: and another book was opened, which is the book of life: and the dead were judged out of those things which were written in the books, according to their works.*

Remember, works won't matter if you are not in the Book of Life. The only reason works are mentioned here is because the saints are at the White Throne Judgment.

(Hebrews 9:27-28) [27]*And as it is appointed unto men once to die, but after this the judgment.* [28]*So Christ was once offered to bear the sins of many; and unto them that look for him shall he appear the second time without sin unto salvation.*

Those without sin will be in the Book of Life and will be judged by their works.

ETERNITY

After the White Throne Judgment, the saints will be moving into the New Jerusalem to live for eternity.

(Revelation 21:2) [2]*And I John saw the holy city, new Jerusalem, coming down from God out of heaven, prepared as a bride adorned for her husband.*

Jesus told His disciples He was going to go and prepare a place for them and He would come back to stay with them.

> (John 14:2-3) [2]*In my Father's house are many mansions: if it were not so, I would have told you. I go to prepare a place for you.* [3]*And if I go and prepare a place for you, I will come again, and receive you unto myself; that where I am, there ye may be also.*

What a place He prepared, not only for His disciples, but for us as well.

> (Revelation 21:16-17) [16]*And the city lieth foursquare, and the length is as large as the breadth: and he measured the city with the reed, twelve thousand furlongs. The length and the breadth and the height of it are equal.* [17]*And he measured the wall thereof, an hundred and forty and four cubits, according to the measure of a man, that is, of the angel.*

The New Jerusalem is 1500 miles long, 1500 miles wide and 1500 miles high. The walls around the city are approx 216 feet high. The city is spectacularly adorned. To see the rest of the description read the Book of the Revelation Chapter 21.

SUMMARY

Do you remember what this chapter is all about, 'Saints in Heaven'? Who have we seen in Heaven in the Book of the Revelation? First, we saw the twenty-four elders. Then we saw the dead souls from the Tribulation. At the end of the Tribulation, we saw the Rapture of the 'dead in Christ'. Those from before the Tribulation and those saints still alive at the end of the Tribulation will be taken to Heaven. After that time there are no more saints dead or alive on earth. This last group will only have about forty-five days in Heaven before they will be part of the armies of Heaven during the second coming.

There are only a few saints going to Heaven before the Tribulation. They are called elders and there are only twenty-four of them. You would have to be one of the spiritual giants to make this group.

The saints that die during the Tribulation period will be allowed directly into Heaven. They will have overcome the beast, maintained their testimony of Jesus Christ, and will not have worshiped the beast or received his mark. All Saints that die before the Tribulation will have to wait until the Rapture at the end of the Tribulation. At the end of the Tribulation, there will be a reaping of the earth. Those found to have overcome and maintained their testimony and not received the mark and not worshiped the beast will be reaped (Raptured) and will join the army from Heaven. The dead in Christ from before the Tribulation will also be part of the Rapture.

I once had a person tell me they didn't care if they have to clean the streets of glory with a toothbrush as long as they get there. There is only one way to get to eternity with God and that is faith in Jesus Christ. Your rewards in eternity with God will be based on your works performed after your salvation.

If you have an opportunity for works and have none, you may not make it to Heaven.

That concludes the study on saints in Heaven.

Chapter 5 Introduction to Tribulation Sequences

Sequences of the Book of the Revelation

The Book of the Revelation, as was pointed out earlier, is not a sequential history book. It has sequences that parallel each other in time. Most of these sequences contain information not found in the other sequences, but some share similar information. In most cases they are separated in Scripture by commentaries on various issues.

All of this makes understanding the book very difficult. In Daniel 12:4, an angel told Daniel *"But thou, O Daniel, shut up the words, and seal the book, even to the time of the end: many shall run to and fro, and knowledge shall increase"*. What did he mean?

Over time knowledge of history and technology has increased and will continue to increase, making the prophecy come to life. Many historical references have past and we see them clearly. However, we don't have the ability to see the future. The Book of the Revelation gives us a glimpse into the future, but because of the language and technological barriers, much of the prophecy is still unclear.

The best we can do with those areas is to rightly divide them to make it easier to comprehend when events will take place.

As near as I can tell, the Book of the Revelations has six sequences which lead to Armageddon or include events just before Armageddon. The list below gives the chapters and verses of the sequences leading to Armageddon.

Book of Seals (Seals 1- 6)	Chapter 6:17
Trumpets (1- 6)	Chapter 9:14-16
Two Witnesses	Chapter 11:15
Rapture	Chapter 14:19-20
Bowls (1-6)	Chapter 16:16
Army from Heaven	Chapter 19:15

We will study each of these sequences individually and in as much detail as we can. As was pointed out above, there are areas where we don't have enough information to be able to **know** what they mean. Daniel said 'knowledge shall increase'. I am confident as the end times draw near, we will be able to **know** what every part of this prophecy means.

Now let's move on to the first Sequence leading to Armageddon. It is the Book of Seven Seals.

Chapter 6 SEQUENCE 1
THE BOOK OF SEVEN SEALS

The Book of the Revelation 6:1-17

We will open this chapter with a question. Is the Book of Seals the same book referred to in Daniel 12:4 that he was told to seal up until the time of the end? We aren't given enough information to make this determination with any degree of certainty. We can say it probably is the same book based on the statement in Daniel 12:4, "*But thou, O Daniel, shut up the words, and seal the book, even to the time of the end: many shall run to and fro, and knowledge shall be increased*". The book is to be sealed until the time of the end. It also says the understanding will come at the end times as "*knowledge shall be increased*". Obviously, at the time of this righting we are not at the end. There are far too many areas we do not understand.

The Book of Seals starts off with four seals and with four horsemen. The significance of the four horses and their colors would be pure conjecture, so we won't cover them here.

The horsemen we will discuss.

The first horseman on a white horse is said to have a bow and a crown on his head and is conquering to conquer (Revelation 6:2). The second horseman on a red horse is given power to take peace from the earth (Revelation 6:4). The third horseman is on a black horse and appears to represent a famine (Revelation 6:5-6). The fourth horseman on a pale horse is named Death and hell followed him. He was given power over one fourth of the earth to kill with sword, hunger, and with death, and with the beasts of the earth. The fourth of the earth is probably referring to the saints on earth. We will see later they are too many to number (Revelation 6:7-8).

The description of the fourth horseman seems to tell us that all four are connected and in reality, they are the same person or authority? They appear to represent an actual progression of events? They appear to be directly connected:

1. Conquering in a rise to power
2. Taking over the reins of the entire world
3. Use of power to manipulate the world's food supply to create famines
4. Droughts from the plagues of the two witnesses will also create famines
5. Killing the saints on a worldwide basis

Using these points, we can make a strong case the four horsemen are from the Tribulation period and represent the fourth beast, the antichrist and the false prophet as told to us by Daniel.

> (Daniel 7:23-25) [23]"*The fourth beast shall be the fourth kingdom upon earth, which shall be diverse from all kingdoms, and shall devour the whole earth, and shall tread it down, and break it in pieces.* [24]*And the ten horns out of this kingdom are ten kings that shall arise: and another shall rise after them; and he shall be diverse from the first, and he shall subdue three kings.* [25]*And he shall speak great words against the most High, and shall wear out the saints of the most High, and think to change times and laws: and they shall be given into his hand until a time and times and the dividing of time.*"

In addition to Daniel, Jesus Christ gave us an outline of the future events in Matthew 24. So, when all else fails, I go back to the supreme authority for an absolute. If Jesus said it, that settles it.

In Matthew 24:6-7, we are told "*nation will rise against nation, and kingdom against kingdom.*" "*There shall be famines and pestilences and earthquakes in diverse places.*"

The third horseman text also states, "*see thou hurt not the oil and the wine.*" (Revelation 6:6.) Some say this is because the wealthy are not hurt significantly by famine and wars. They still live in opulence. In the time of John, the oil and wine were expensive and in some cases were even used as currency or barter items. So, here again we are not given enough information to know why he said not to hurt the oil or the wine.

The fifth seal would indicate seals one through four extend into the Tribulation (Revelation 6:9-11). The fifth seal places us in the middle of the Great Tribulation.

> (Revelation 6:9-11) 9*When He opened the fifth seal, I saw under the altar the souls of those who had been slain for the word of God and for the testimony which they held.* 10 *And they cried with a loud voice, saying, "How long, O Lord, holy and true, until You judge and avenge our blood on those who dwell on the earth?"* 11 *Then a white robe was given to each of them; and it was said to them that they should rest a little while longer, until both the number of their fellow servants and their brethren, who would be killed as they were, was completed.*

This seal tells us of the souls of people killed during the Tribulation period. It isn't explained specifically here, but in the Book of the Revelation 7:9-17 it is made clear to us.

(Revelation 7:9-17) 9 *After these things I looked, and behold, a great multitude which no one could number, of all nations, tribes, peoples, and tongues, standing before the throne and before the Lamb, clothed with white robes, with palm branches in their hands,* 10 *and crying out with a loud voice, saying, "Salvation belongs to our God who sits on the throne, and to the Lamb!"* 11 *All the angels stood around the throne and the elders and the four living creatures, and fell on their faces before the throne and worshiped God,* 12 *saying: "Amen! Blessing and glory and wisdom, Thanksgiving and honor and power and might, Be to our God forever and ever. Amen."* 13 *Then one of the elders answered, saying to me, "Who are these arrayed in white robes, and where did they come from?"* 14 *And I said to him, "Sir, you know." So he said to me, "These are the ones who come out of the great tribulation, and washed their robes and made them white in the blood of the Lamb.* 15 *Therefore they are before the throne of God, and serve Him day and night in His temple. And He who sits on the throne will dwell among them.* 16 *They shall neither hunger anymore nor thirst anymore; the sun shall not strike them, nor any heat;* 17 *for the Lamb who is in the midst of the throne will shepherd them and lead them to living fountains of waters. And God will wipe away every tear from their eyes."*

As a matter of clarification, when we were first given a verbal picture of Heaven and the throne room, there was no reference to any souls or multitudes of people in Heaven or around the throne. The only possible reference to humans is the 24 elders. We are not told who the 24 elders are. Some have tried to imply the 24 elders represent a multitude. I fail to see how they can make this claim. The number of the elders is made clear. They are a specific number. I believe the number of souls before the throne is given as a great multitude which no one could number to let us know the rapture doesn't happen before the Tribulation starts.

If there were no souls under the altar when John arrived in the throne room, then we can say the souls under the altar in the Book of the Revelation Chapter 6 were from the Tribulation and become a part of the multitude before the throne in the Book of the Revelation Chapter 7.

For those who don't understand how washing in blood can make their robes white, it is the Blood of Jesus Christ that removes the dark stain of sin in our lives.

Now we are ready to look at the sixth seal. Chapter 6:12-17 of the Book of the Revelation.

> (Revelation 6:12-17) [12]*I looked when He opened the sixth seal, and behold, there was a great earthquake; and the sun became black as sackcloth of hair, and the moon became like blood.* [13] *And the stars of heaven fell to the earth, as a fig tree drops its late figs when it is shaken by a mighty wind.* [14] *Then the sky receded as a scroll when it is rolled up, and every mountain and island was moved out of its place.* [15] *And the kings of the earth, the great men, the rich men, the commanders, the mighty men, every slave and every free man, hid themselves in the caves and in the rocks of the mountains,* [16] *and said to the mountains and rocks, "Fall on us and hide us from the face of Him who sits on the throne and from the wrath of the Lamb!* [17] *For the great day of His wrath has come, and who is able to stand?"*

This is clearly what Christ's prophecy in Matthew 24:29 refers to.

(Matthew 24:29) [29]"*Immediately after the tribulation of those days the sun will be darkened, and the moon will not give its light; the stars will fall from heaven, and the powers of the heavens will be shaken.*

Are these events the result of a supernatural event or a cataclysmic earth event? Could the earthquake, sun blackened, moon turned to blood be the result of a super volcano?

Could the '*stars falling from heaven*', '*heaven departed as a scroll and every mountain and island moved out of their place*' be the result of a large meteor shower, a comet, or an asteroid shower? In Chapter 19:3 of the Book of the Revelation we are told "*...and her smoke rose up for ever and ever*". If this implies Jerusalem was destroyed by a nuclear blast, it could explain, "*a great earthquake; and the sun became black as sackcloth of hair, and the moon became like blood.* [13] *And the stars of heaven fell to the earth, as a fig tree drops its late figs when it is shaken by a mighty wind.* [14] *Then the sky receded as a scroll when it is rolled up, and every mountain and island was moved out of its place*" (Revelation 6:12-14).

I guess we will find out the truth when this actually happens. If someone tells you they are this or that, they are guessing. There isn't enough information given to us to make an informed decision. In reality it doesn't matter in the overall study. It should suffice to know, these events referred to in the sixth seal will occur after the end of the Great Tribulation as told in Matthew 24:29.

After the period of, '*the sun will be darkened, and the moon will not give its light; the stars will fall from heaven, and the powers of the heavens will be shaken.*' We move into Armageddon. In Matthew 24: 30, Jesus tells us after the Tribulation and after the supernatural events of the Book of the Revelation 6:12 and Matthew 24:29 '*then shall appear the sign of the Son of man in heaven.*'

(Matthew 24:30-31) [30]*And then shall appear the sign of the Son of man in heaven: and then shall all the tribes of the earth mourn, and they shall see the Son of man coming in the clouds of heaven with power and great glory.* [31]*And he shall send his angels with a great sound of a trumpet, and they shall gather together his elect from the four winds, from one end of heaven to the other.*

This is the second coming of Christ with the armies of Heaven. It is important to note the elect are gathered from one end of Heaven to the other. He is not gathering from the earth.

There can be no doubt the sequence of the Book of Seals leads to Armageddon and beyond. That concludes the study of our first sequence to Armageddon.

Chapter 7 SEQUENCE 2

Seven Trumpets

The Book of the Revelation 9:14-16

Tribulation or Wrath of God

Before we study the actions of the Trumpets, let's establish when they bring their actions upon the earth.

In the study of the sixth seal of the Book of Seals, we saw the association with Matthew 24: 29.

> (Revelation 6:12-13) [12]*And I beheld when he had opened the sixth seal, and, lo, there was a great earthquake; and the sun became black as sackcloth of hair, and the moon became as blood;* [13]*And the stars of heaven fell unto the earth, even as a fig tree casteth her untimely figs, when she is shaken of a mighty wind.*

> Compare this Scripture to Matthew 24:29.

> (Matthew 24:29) [29]*Immediately after the tribulation of those days shall the sun be darkened, and the moon shall not give her light, and the stars shall fall from heaven, and the powers of the heavens shall be shaken:*

They are virtually the same. At the end of the Tribulation there will be a period of natural disasters. This period will come after the Tribulation and before Armageddon. Jesus tells us in Matthew 24:30.

> (Matthew 24:30) [30]*And then shall appear the sign of the Son of man in heaven: and then shall all the tribes of the earth mourn, and they shall see*

the Son of man coming in the clouds of heaven with power and great glory.

We go from after the Tribulation of those days (Matthew 24:29) where we have the natural disasters to the sign of the Son of man appearing (Matthew 24:30). During that time in-between, we have the time of the sixth seal which is the same as the Matthew 24:29. It is important for us to read all of the sixth seal.

(Revelation 6:12-17) 12 *And I beheld when he had opened the sixth seal, and, lo, there was a great earthquake; and the sun became black as sackcloth of hair, and the moon became as blood;* 13 *And the stars of heaven fell unto the earth, even as a fig tree casteth her untimely figs, when she is shaken of a mighty wind.* 14 *And the heaven departed as a scroll when it is rolled together; and every mountain and island were moved out of their places.* 15 *And the kings of the earth, and the great men, and the rich men, and the chief captains, and the mighty men, and every bondman, and every free man, hid themselves in the dens and in the rocks of the mountains;* 16 *And said to the mountains and rocks, Fall on us, and hide us from the face of him that sitteth on the throne, and from the wrath of the Lamb:* 17 *For the great day of his wrath is come; and who shall be able to stand?*

In the Book of the Revelation 6:12–13 we see the connection to Matthew 24:29 which will take place after the Tribulation. In the Book of the Revelation 6:17 we see the difference that is taking place. In the Book of the Revelation 6:17 we see the movement to the wrath of God. Do not confuse this with Armageddon.

In the book of Job we were given an example of the Tribulation. In the case of Job, God ALLOWED Satan to test Job and put him through a period of tribulation. Job overcame the tribulation brought against him. As a result of Job's overcoming, God not only restored him to his former status but gave him much more. This is what will happen to the saints that go through the Great Tribulation. God will allow them to be tested by Satan through the antichrist. For those that overcome, great will be their reward in Heaven. At the end of the Great Tribulation, the saints alive and dead will be raptured, for they are not to suffer the wrath of God.

The following Scriptures tell us, the saints are to be kept from the wrath of God. These are often misinterpreted to mean we are to be kept from the Great Tribulation. As we have seen, this is not so. There are two separate times of distress. There is the Great Tribulation which is Satan's persecution of the saints and then there is the period of the wrath of God which is God's persecution of those that persecuted His people.

We have Scriptures that tell us we are saved from His wrath and we have Scriptures that tell us His wrath is for the disobedient:

> (Romans 5:9) [9]*Much more then, being now justified by his blood, we shall be saved from wrath through him.*
>
> (Ephesians 5:6) [6]*Let no man deceive you with vain words: for because of these things cometh the wrath of God upon the children of disobedience.*
>
> (1Thessalonians 1:10) [10]*And to wait for his Son from heaven, whom he raised from the dead, even Jesus, which delivered us from the wrath to come.*
>
> (1Thessalonians 5:9) [9]*For God hath not appointed us to wrath, but to obtain salvation by our Lord Jesus Christ,*

The saints have not been appointed to suffer God's wrath. We are to suffer tribulation. That places the Rapture between the Great Tribulation and the wrath of God. There will still be some saints alive at the end of the Great Tribulation. We are told in I Thessalonians that those saints alive at the time of the Rapture will be raised after the dead.

> (1Thessalonians 4:16-17) 16*For the Lord himself shall descend from heaven with a shout, with the voice of the archangel, and with the trump of God: and the dead in Christ shall rise first:* 17*Then we which are alive and remain shall be caught up together with them in the clouds, to meet the Lord in the air: and so shall we ever be with the Lord.*

We do have a Scripture that says we are to be kept from the hour of temptation which is to come upon the entire world. Is this referring to the Great Tribulation? I don't think so. There are too many Scriptures that tell us that we are to endure tribulation. Take a look at the life of Paul.

I hope I haven't confused you with this. Let me summarize.

1. Those of us alive at the time of the Great Tribulation will go through it.
2. At the end of the Great Tribulation at the last trump, the saints, dead and alive, will be raptured.
3. Then there will be a period of God's wrath upon the earth.
4. Then Armageddon comes.

Abomination of Desolation

What triggers this transition from the Tribulation to the wrath of God? What is it that will cause God to remove all of His people from the earth and to bring His wrath upon the earth? We see it prophesied in Daniel and in the Gospel of Mark.

It is the Abomination of Desolation. This was spoken of in Daniel 11. It is the setting up of the image (Idol) of the antichrist in the Temple of God in Jerusalem. At this point God removes His two witnesses and the remaining saints from the earth. This is the tipping point of Gods patience. God has had enough and brings His wrath upon those that dared to come against His people. It is the Abomination of Desolation. Daniel prophesied about it in Daniel 9:27; 11:31; 12:11.

> (Daniel 11:31) [31]*And arms shall stand on his part, and they shall pollute the sanctuary of strength, and shall take away the daily sacrifice, and they shall place the abomination that maketh desolate.*

Daniel tells us where the Abomination of Desolation takes place. He tells us they will pollute the sanctuary by placing the abomination in the sanctuary.

> (Mark 13:14) [14]*But when ye shall see the abomination of desolation, spoken of by Daniel the prophet, standing where it ought not, (let him that readeth understand,) then let them that be in Judaea flee to the mountains:*

What is this abomination? We are not specifically told what the abomination is, but based on Daniel 11:31 we can make a strong case for it to be the image of the beast. It will '*pollute the Sanctuary*' when '*they place the abomination that maketh desolate.*'

We then see in the Book of the Revelation 13:14 the antichrist will seek the annihilation of worshippers of God and will seek to be worshiped. He will pollute the sanctuary of the temple of God by having an image (idol) of himself placed in the temple of God in Jerusalem.

> (Revelation 13:14-15) [14]*And deceiveth them that dwell on the earth by the means of those miracles which he had power to do in the sight of the beast; saying to them that dwell on the earth, that they should make an image to the beast, which had the wound by a sword, and did live.* [15]*And he had power to give life unto the image of the beast, that the image of the beast should both speak, and cause that as many as would not worship the image of the beast should be killed.*
>
> It isn't a good idea to place one's self above God.

Overview of Trumpets

Now we will look at where the Trumpets fit into all of this.

Time of the Seven Trumpets

> (Revelation *8:1-2)* [1]*And when he had opened the seventh seal, there was silence in heaven about the space of half an hour.* [2]*And I saw the seven angels which stood before God; and to them were given seven trumpets.*

These verses appear to place the seven trumpets after the seventh seal. Not so. The events of the seven trumpets cannot take place after the seventh seal, since they happen during the Great Tribulation. At the time of the seventh seal, the Great Tribulation is over. We will see in the fifth trumpet the bottomless pit is unlocked and opened. This is when the antichrist is released out of the bottomless pit. In the Book of the Revelation 11:7 we are told the antichrist ascended out of the bottomless pit. He couldn't have ascended out of the bottomless pit until it was unlocked by Satan. Satan unlocked the bottomless pit at the time of the fifth trumpet. This would have to have been before the Great Tribulation. We will pursue this further later in this chapter.

Purposes of the Trumpets

Trumpets have been used throughout the Bible for various reasons. The main purposes have been:

- For music
- For praise to God
- As an alarm of a pending attack
- As a call to Arms
- As a call to assemble
- As a call to appear before God

The seven trumpets used in the Book of the Revelation are for two reasons:

- Trumps 1-4 are a warning of impending attacks from the skies.
- Trump 5 is a warning of impending danger from Satan being cast down to earth.
- Trump 6 is a warning of a major military attack from the East.
- Trump 7 is a call to come to God.
- Trumpets 1 – 4 are found in the Book of the Revelation Chapter 8.

First Trumpet: Vegetation Struck

(Revelation 8:7) [7]*The first angel sounded: And hail and fire followed, mingled with blood, and they were thrown to the earth. And a third of the trees were burned up, and all green grass was burned up.*

Second Trumpet: The Seas Struck

(Revelation 8:8-9) [8]*Then the second angel sounded: And something like a great mountain burning with fire was thrown into the sea, and a third of the sea became blood.* [9] *And a third of the living creatures in the sea died, and a third of the ships were destroyed.*

Third Trumpet: The Rivers & Springs Struck

(Revelation 8:10-11) [10]*Then the third angel sounded: And a great star fell from heaven, burning like a torch, and it fell on a third of the rivers and on the springs of water.* [11] *The name of the star is Wormwood. A third of the waters became wormwood, and many men died from the water, because it was made bitter.*

Fourth Trumpet: The Heavens Struck

(Revelation 8:12) [12]*Then the fourth angel sounded: And a third of the sun was struck, a third of the moon, and a third of the stars, so that a third of them were darkened. A third of the day did not shine, and likewise the night.*

These first four Trumpets appear to be connected. They all show effects of a single event. A third of the trees & green grass are burned up. A third of the sea became blood. A third of the waters became wormwood. A third of the sun was struck. A third of the moon and a third of the stars were darkened. These catastrophes were caused by hail and fire, a great mountain burning with fire, and a great star falling from Heaven, burning.

Will it be a comet, a meteor, an asteroid shower, or a supernatural event? We don't know. All of these are plausible. With God's control of the universe, any or all may be true.

Question, does this refer to the entire Earth, or just to Israel? We aren't told where this happens, but we know this happens before the Great Tribulation, since the antichrist has not ascended out of the bottomless pit.

The next two trumpets are found in the Book of the Revelation Chapter 9.

Fifth Trumpet: The Locusts from the Bottomless Pit

> (Revelation *9:1-3)* [1]*Then the fifth angel sounded: And I saw a star fallen from heaven to the earth. To him was given the key to the bottomless pit.* [2] *And he opened the bottomless pit, and smoke arose out of the pit like the smoke of a great furnace. So the sun and the air were darkened because of the smoke of the pit.* [3] *Then out of the smoke locusts came upon the earth. And to them was given power, as the scorpions of the earth have power.*

Here again we see Satan being kicked out of Heaven and forced to reside on Earth. His first act is to release his demons from the bottomless pit. One of them will become the antichrist. We are told in the Book of the Revelation 11:7 the antichrist, the same one who kills the two witnesses, ascended out of the bottomless pit. This places the fifth trumpet before the Tribulation.

The bottomless pit was locked until Satan was kicked out of Heaven and he unlocked it, releasing the antichrist.

After ascending out of the bottomless pit, the antichrist rises to become the worldwide leader.

Three and a half years before the Great Tribulation, the antichrist negotiates the Seven-year treaty with Israel.

How long before the Great Tribulation did the antichrist ascend out of the bottomless pit? We aren't given that information. It had to be before the Seven-year treaty was signed.

Now let's deal with the locusts from the bottomless pit.

> (Revelation *9:4-11)* [4]*They were commanded not to harm the grass of the earth, or any green thing, or any tree, but only those men who do not have the seal of God on their foreheads.* [5]*And they were not given authority to kill them, but to torment them for five months. Their torment was like the torment of a scorpion when it strikes a man.* [6] *In those days men will seek death and will not find it; they will desire to die, and death will flee from them.* [7]*The shape of the locusts was like horses prepared for battle. On their heads were crowns of something like gold, and their faces were like the faces of men.* [8] *They had hair like women's hair, and their teeth were like lions' teeth.* [9] *And they had breastplates like breastplates of iron, and the sound of their wings was like the sound of chariots with many horses running into battle.* [10] *They had tails like scorpions, and there were stings in their tails. Their power was to hurt men five months.* [11] *And they had as king over them the angel of the bottomless pit, whose name in Hebrew is Abaddon, but in Greek he has the name Apollyon.*

We don't have enough information to know who or what the locusts are. This is one of those areas where the knowledge has not presented itself. So, let's put together some hypotheticals.

First, let's look at the king over them, Abaddon/Apollyon. Abaddon is a destroying angel. Apollyon is a destroyer like Satan. Is the king over them Satan or is it the antichrist? Is there an evil hierarchy like a regular kingdom? Is Satan the lord of the dark side and the antichrist a king of the dark side? I believe Abaddon and Apollyon are referring to Satan.

Now, let's look at the locusts. Obviously, they are not locusts as we know them. Do the locusts represent an army of the antichrist? If they come from the bottomless pit they are most certainly demons in the service of Satan. Regardless of whom they work for, they are not human. However, they could possess humans. More importantly they could possess a military force.

This Trumpet poses a couple of issues in relation to timing.

First, is the release of the antichrist from the bottomless pit? In the Book of the Revelation Chapter 11, we are told the antichrist came out of the bottomless pit.

> (Revelation 11:7) [7]*And when they shall have finished their testimony, the beast that ascendeth out of the bottomless pit shall make war against them, and shall overcome them, and kill them.*

This Scripture is referring to the antichrist. If the antichrist ascended out of the bottomless pit and the bottomless pit was locked until the fifth trumpet, then the fifth trumpet has to be before the Seven-year treaty is signed.

Our second question is what or who is the star fallen from Heaven with the key to the bottomless pit? This is answered in the text of verse 11, *And they had as king over them the angel of the bottomless pit, whose name in Hebrew is Abaddon, but in Greek he has the name Apollyon. In the Greek language this is a name given to Satan.*

The third question is what is the bottomless pit?

We are not given a specific determination of the bottomless pit anywhere in Scripture. However; in the Book of the Revelation 20:3, we are told Satan is bound in the bottomless pit for 1,000 years. That would lead me to believe the bottomless pit could be Hell (Hades). Hell isn't done away with until after the Great White Throne Judgment at the end of the Millennium.

The fourth question is when is this event that darkened the sun?

We don't have enough information to determine exactly when this happens but we know if it is connected with the release of the antichrist from the bottomless pit, it has to be before the signing of the Seven-year treaty. This would preclude it from being associated with the sun darkening prophesied in Matthew 24 and the Book of the Revelation 6.

Questions 5 – 14 deal with the locusts and cannot be answered with certainty.

5. What are these locusts with power as the scorpion has power?
6. How can locusts be shaped like horses prepared for battle?
7. How can locusts have crowns of something like gold?
8. How can locusts have faces like men?
9. How can locusts have hair like a woman?
10. How can locusts have teeth like a lion?

11. How can locusts have breastplates of iron?
12. How can locusts have wings that sound like many horses running to battle?
13. How can locusts have tails like scorpions?
14. How can locusts have stings in their tails?

The locusts are obviously not locusts as we understand them. Let's take a few of these to help narrow down the description. Let's make an assumption and then plug in some details.

We know there is no way John had the technical understanding of weapons of warfare 2000 years into his future. So, let's assume the locusts are actually some sort of weapons system of today or not too far into the future. Could he be describing something like an attack helicopter? Remember, John has never seen or heard of such a thing and has no technical language to describe modern technology.

Photo from Wikipedia Online

Remember this is hypothetical and is not meant to be a direct interpretation of Scripture. The basic shape of a helicopter is that of a horse, including a tail extending past the rear wheels. Think of the Apache helicopter.

The Scripture says the wings sound like many horses running to battle. Anyone that has heard a jet helicopter knows this could be interpreted as the sound of many horses running to battle.

They have breastplates of iron. This would describe the skin of a helicopter. They have teeth of a lion. Could this be the intake of the jet engines? They have faces like men. The faces of the helicopter pilots would be visible through the canopy. They have crowns of something like gold. Could this be the pilot's helmet? How can they have stings in their tails? There are a couple of possibilities. One could be a rear weapon of some sort.

Next, let's consider the mission. They are to hurt men and nothing else for five months. Men will be tormented and seek death, but not die. Could this represent the use of chemical weapons? If a helicopter was used to spray the chemical weapons, you would want to eliminate the possibility of the helicopter getting coated and the pilot getting exposed to the chemical. That would necessitate the chemical being released in the area of the tail.

Also, this theory is supported by the next question. How can they torment for five months? Chemical weapons can be designed to do this in today's world.

This leaves the hair like a woman. This could be the appearance of the rotors of the helicopter. Remember this analysis is all theory, not Scripture.

Who are those without the mark of God on their forehead? It might be easier to say, who has the mark of God in their forehead?

> (Revelation 7:2-8) 2 *Then I saw another angel ascending from the east,
> *having the seal of the living God. And he cried with a loud voice to the*
> *four angels to whom it was granted to harm the earth and the sea,* 3
> *saying, "Do not harm the earth, the sea, or the trees till we have sealed the*
> *servants of our God on their foreheads."* 4 *And I heard the number of*
> *those who were sealed. One hundred and forty-four thousand of all the*
> *tribes of the children of Israel were sealed:* 5 *of the tribe of Judah twelve*
> *thousand were sealed; of the tribe of Reuben twelve thousand were sealed;*
> *of the tribe of Gad twelve thousand were sealed;* 6 *of the tribe of Asher*

twelve thousand were sealed; of the tribe of Naphtali twelve thousand were sealed; of the tribe of Manasseh twelve thousand were sealed; [7] *of the tribe of Simeon twelve thousand were sealed; of the tribe of Levi twelve thousand were sealed; of the tribe of Issachar twelve thousand were sealed;* [8] *of the tribe of Zebulun twelve thousand were sealed; of the tribe of Joseph twelve thousand were sealed; of the tribe of Benjamin twelve thousand were sealed.*

So the answer to who has the mark of God on their forehead is 144,000 Israelites, marked before the Great Tribulation is allowed to start. Why are they selected for exclusion? We get that from the Book of the Revelation 14:4-5.

(Revelation 14:4-5) [4]*"These are the ones who were not defiled with women, for they are virgins. These are the ones who follow the Lamb wherever He goes. These were redeemed from among men, being first fruits to God and to the Lamb.* [5] *And in their mouth was found no deceit, for they are without fault before the throne of God".*

We can be relatively certain; the army, represented by the locusts, is not the invading army of 200,000,000 from the east. They are to hurt men for five months. They are not sent to destroy one-third of mankind. Now we move on to the last warning of an impending attack.

Sixth Trumpet: The Angels from the Euphrates

(Revelation *9:13-21)* [13]*Then the sixth angel sounded: And I heard a voice from the four horns of the golden altar which is before God,* [14] *saying to the sixth angel who had the trumpet, "Release the four angels who are bound at the great river Euphrates."* [15] *So the four angels, who had been prepared for the hour and day and month and year, were released to kill a third of mankind.* [16] *Now the number of the army of the horsemen was two hundred million; I heard the number of them.* [17] *And thus I saw the horses in the vision: those who sat on them had breastplates of fiery red, hyacinth blue, and sulfur yellow; and the heads of the horses were like the heads of lions; and out of their mouths came fire, smoke, and brimstone.* [18] *By these three plagues a third of mankind was killed—by the fire and the smoke and the brimstone which came out of their mouths.* [19] *For their power*[a] *is in their mouth and in their tails; for their tails are like serpents, having heads; and with them they do harm.* [20] *But the rest of mankind, who were not killed by these plagues, did not repent of the works of their hands, that they should not worship demons, and idols of gold, silver, brass, stone, and wood, which can neither see nor hear nor walk.* [21] *And they did not repent of their murders or their sorceries or their sexual immorality or their thefts.*

I have two questions.

1. Where does this 200,000,000-man army come from; and where are they going?

   (Revelation 16:12,16) [12]*And the sixth angel poured out his vial upon the great river Euphrates; and the water thereof was dried up, that the way of the kings of the east might be prepared*

   [16]*And he gathered them together into a place called in the Hebrew tongue Armageddon.*

   We are told the Euphrates is dried up to make way for the kings of the east and they are headed to Armageddon. So, we have four nations from the east of Israel and they are going to end up at Armageddon.

2. If the result is to have 1/3 of mankind killed, who are the 1/3 of mankind? On October 21, 2009, the world's population was 6,791,903,951; United States' population was 307,748,629, and Israel's population was 7,411,000. One-third of the world's population would be 2,263,967,984.

   Could a 200 million-man army kill over 2 billion people? My guess is they are going after Israel. They kill one-third (2,470,333) of the Israelis; those that haven't fled into the wilderness. Then the 200,000,000-man army is destroyed by God at Armageddon.

   (Revelation 17:16-18) [16]*And the ten horns which thou sawest upon the beast, these shall hate the whore, and shall make her desolate and naked, and shall eat her flesh, and burn her with fire.* [17]*For God hath put in their hearts to fulfil his will, and to agree, and give their kingdom unto the beast, until the words of God shall be fulfilled.* [18]*And the woman which thou sawest is that great city, which reigneth over the kings of the earth.*

These great armies are merely doing Gods bidding. The great whore is referring to Israel and more specifically Jerusalem which by that time has become the seat of the antichrist from which he rules the world. Some say the 'armies of the East' is referring to disgruntled nations from the East coming to destroy the antichrist. This is possible, but the Bible says they are headed to Armageddon.

Remember at this point they are headed to Armageddon, but they are not there. One more Trumpet to Go.

Seventh Trumpet: Mystery of God Should Be Finished

(Revelation 10:7) [7]*But in the days of the voice of the seventh angel, when he shall begin to sound, the mystery of God should be finished, as he hath declared to his servants the prophets.*

(Revelation 11:15-18) [15]*And the seventh angel sounded; and there were great voices in heaven, saying, The kingdoms of this world are become the kingdoms of our Lord, and of his Christ; and he shall reign for ever and ever.* [16]*And the four and twenty elders, which sat before God on their seats, fell upon their faces, and worshipped God,* [17]*Saying, We give thee thanks, O LORD God Almighty, which art, and wast, and art to come; because thou hast taken to thee thy great power, and hast reigned.* [18]*And the nations were angry, and thy wrath is come, and the time of the dead, that they should be judged, and that thou shouldest give reward unto thy servants the prophets, and to the saints, and them that fear thy name, small and great; and shouldest destroy them which destroy the earth.*

This Trumpet is broken into two parts. The first part is in the Book of the Revelation 10:7. John says, when the seventh angel shall begin to sound the mystery of God should be finished. What mystery should be finished?

(1Timothy 3:16) [16]*And without controversy great is the mystery of godliness: God was manifest in the flesh, justified in the Spirit, seen of angels, preached unto the Gentiles, believed on in the world, received up into glory.*

He is telling us the salvation through Jesus Christ is come to an end. It has fulfilled its purpose and all the saints have been received into Heaven at the time of the Rapture.

The second part of the seventh trump is the end of two separate kingdoms. The kingdoms of Heaven and Earth have become one kingdom of our Lord.

This concludes our study of the Seven Trumpets, the second of our six sequences leading to Armageddon.

Chapter 8 SEQUENCE 3

GODS TWO WITNESSES

The Book of the Revelation 11:3-13

We are told God will send two witnesses to Earth for the same period of time as the Tribulation period. They are to be dressed in sackcloth, which is a poor man's clothing, implying they will not be big-time leaders. They will be ministering on the level of the common man.

> (Revelation 11:3-4) [3]*And I will give power to my two witnesses, and they will prophesy one thousand two hundred and sixty days, clothed in sackcloth."*[4]*These are the two olive trees and the two lamp stands standing before the God of the earth.*

This verse (4) refers back to John's visit to the throne room in Heaven, where he saw, "*seven lamps of fire burning before the throne*" (Revelation 4:5).

Even though these two witnesses are meek and contrite and clothed in sackcloth, they are not defenseless. God has equipped them with the ability to defend their selves, as well as to bring plagues against nations. They will have power over all the plagues, drought, water to blood, pestilence, etc.

> (Revelation 11:5-6) [5]*And if anyone wants to harm them, fire proceeds from their mouth and devours their enemies. And if anyone wants to harm them, he must be killed in this manner.* [6] *These have power to shut heaven, so that no rain falls in the days of their prophecy; and they have*

power over waters to turn them to blood, and to strike the earth with all plagues, as often as they desire.

When they have completed their ministry, God will allow the antichrist to kill them. The antichrist will not allow them to be removed from the street where he has killed them. They will lie in the street for 3-1/2 days and will be seen by the entire world. Apparently, the antichrist will allow this exhibition to be televised around the world. There will be rejoicing over the death of the two witnesses because of the torment they brought.

Here again we have mention of the *great city*.

(Revelation *11:7-10)* [7]*When they finish their (1260 days) testimony, the beast that ascends out of the bottomless pit (antichrist) will make war against them, overcome them, and kill them.* [8] *And their dead bodies will lie in the street of the great city which spiritually is called Sodom and Egypt, where also our Lord was crucified.* [9] *Then those from the peoples, tribes, tongues, and nations will see their dead bodies three-and-a-half days, and not allow their dead bodies to be put into graves.* [10] *And those who dwell on the earth will rejoice over them, make merry, and send gifts to one another, because these two prophets tormented those who dwell on the earth.*

Some believe the two witnesses will be killed by Satan. After a fashion they are correct. Actually they are killed by the beast that ascends out of the bottomless pit. Satan didn't ascend out of the bottomless pit. He descended with the key to the bottomless pit and he opened it. Apparently the antichrist is one of Satan's demons and is loosed from the bottomless pit to possess a powerful leader.

There is one more thing about this Scripture that concerns me. It calls for the antichrist to make war against the two witnesses. I looked it up. The word used for war here actually means – busy, noisy activity or commotion. He will actually create a commotion in a public forum and then kill them.

They will lay dead in the street for 3-1/2 days and then they will be brought back to life by the Holy Spirit. Can you imagine the fear generated by this? They lay dead in the street for 3-1/2 days and then they come back to life. They are then taken to Heaven in a cloud. How scary will that be to unbelievers?

Here is a little ditty for you:

- Jesus' ministry was 3-1/2 years
- The two witnesses' ministry, 3-1/2 years
- Jesus returned to Heaven after 3-1/2 days
- The two witnesses return to Heaven after 3-1/2 days

(Revelation 11:11-13) [11]*Now, after the three-and-a-half days the breath of life from God entered them, and they stood on their feet, and great fear fell on those who saw them.* [12]*And they heard a loud voice from heaven saying to them, "Come up here." And they ascended to heaven in a cloud, and their enemies saw them.* [13]*In the same hour there was a great earthquake, and a tenth of the city fell. In the earthquake seven thousand people were killed, and the rest were afraid and gave glory to the God of heaven.*

The two witnesses will be on the earth 1260 days, the exact number of days of the Tribulation. I believe this also signifies the timing of the Rapture of the saints.

We were told the two witnesses will be on Earth 1260 days. That means when they leave it will be the end of the Great Tribulation, which means it's time for the period of the wrath of God.

We are not told the identity of the two witnesses anywhere in the Bible. People have made a good case for the two witnesses to be Elijah and Enoch. They are the only two taken to Heaven without dying first. But, has Elijah already come back and died?

(Matthew 11:11-14) [11]*Verily I say unto you, Among them that are born of women there hath not risen a greater than John the Baptist: notwithstanding he that is least in the kingdom of heaven is greater than he.* [12]*And from the days of John the Baptist until now the kingdom of heaven suffereth violence, and the violent take it by force.* [13]*For all the prophets and the law prophesied until John.* [14]*And if ye will receive it, this is Elias, which was for to come.*

(Matthew *17:10-13)* [10]*And his disciples asked him, saying, Why then say the scribes that Elias must first come?* [11]*And Jesus answered and said unto them, Elias truly shall first come, and restore all things.* [12]*But I say unto you, That Elias is come already, and they knew him not, but have done unto him whatsoever they listed. Likewise shall also the Son of man suffer of them.* [13]*Then the disciples understood that he spake unto them of John the Baptist.*

It appears Jesus is telling us that John the Baptist was in reality Elias (Elijah). If this is what He is saying, there is only one left that has not died. If that is true, then we really don't know who the two witnesses will be.

There is one more possible pairing. In Matthew 17 Jesus was transfigured and met with two saints.

(Matthew 17:1-3) [1]*And after six days Jesus taketh Peter, James, and John his brother, and bringeth them up into an high mountain apart,* [2]*And was transfigured before them: and his face did shine as the sun, and his raiment was white as the light.* [3]*And, behold, there appeared unto them Moses and Elias talking with him.*

Moses and Elias (Elijah) would make a formidable pairing. They have previous experience dealing with plagues, preaching the gospel, and dispensing God's wrath.

When the two witnesses leave the Earth at the end of the Tribulation, it is time for the wrath of God, followed by Armageddon.

Here is a copy of the end time's timeline taken from the chapter on the beast and the false prophet. Let's look at this timeline.

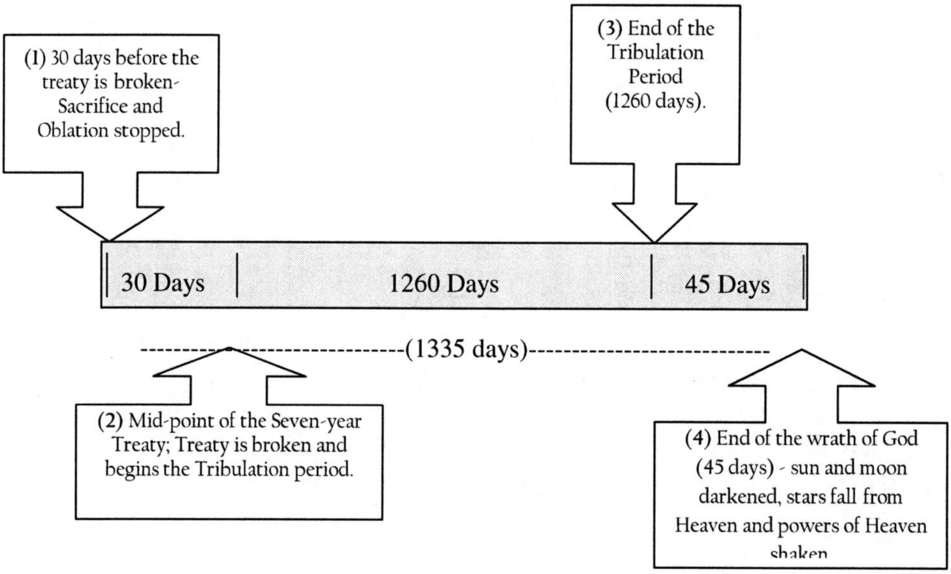
(1) 30 days before the treaty is broken- Sacrifice and Oblation stopped.
(3) End of the Tribulation Period (1260 days).
30 Days
1260 Days
45 Days
(1335 days)
(2) Mid-point of the Seven-year Treaty; Treaty is broken and begins the Tribulation period.
(4) End of the wrath of God (45 days) - sun and moon darkened, stars fall from Heaven and powers of Heaven shaken

This concludes our study on the third sequence leading to Armageddon.

Chapter 9 SEQUENCE 4

THE RAPTURE

The Book of the Revelation 14:14-20

Who goes in the Rapture

We have already looked at the saints that died during the Tribulation. They go directly to Heaven upon their death. So we know they won't need to be raptured. What about the saints that died before the Great Tribulation? They will need a ride in the Rapture.

There will be saints alive at the end of the Tribulation and they will need a ride also. This has been clarified in Scripture.

Yes, those of us alive at the time of the Great Tribulation will go through it. We have been exempted from God's wrath, but we have not been exempted from tribulation. If there is one individual in the New Testament that stands far above all others except Jesus Christ, it has to be Paul. He did more for the spreading of the gospel than any other, from then until now. How is it then that we expect to be exempted from the Tribulation? Who among us dares to think they should be treated better than Paul? Here is a brief account of the tribulations Paul endured in the service of Jesus Christ. These Scriptures are Paul's own words.

> (2Corinthians 11:24-31) 24*Of the Jews five times received I forty stripes save one.* 25*Thrice was I beaten with rods, once was I stoned, thrice I suffered shipwreck, a night and a day I have been in the deep;* 26*In journeyings often, in perils of waters, in perils of robbers, in perils by*

mine own countrymen, in perils by the heathen, in perils in the city, in perils in the wilderness, in perils in the sea, in perils among false brethren;
[27]*In weariness and painfulness, in watchings often, in hunger and thirst, in fastings often, in cold and nakedness.* [28]*Beside those things that are without, that which cometh upon me daily, the care of all the churches.*
[29]*Who is weak, and I am not weak? who is offended, and I burn not?* [30]*If I must needs glory, I will glory of the things which concern mine infirmities.* [31]*The God and Father of our Lord Jesus Christ, which is blessed for evermore, knoweth that I lie not.*

- Stoned once
- Forty lashes five times
- Beaten with rods three times
- Shipwrecked three times
- On the ocean 1-1/2 days

These and more never happened until he was in the service of Jesus Christ. Then in Paul's letter to the Philippians he said this:

(Philippians 1:29) [29]*For unto you it is given in the behalf of Christ, not only to believe on him, but also to suffer for his sake;*

These two Scriptures along with the humiliation, torture and murder of Jesus Christ should make it clear; we are not exempt from tribulation. There is one more Scripture I believe we need to look at. It is normally used for other purposes but I believe it applies here.

(1Thessalonians 4:14-16) [14]*For if we believe that Jesus died and rose again, even so them also which sleep in Jesus will God bring with him.*
[15]*For this we say unto you by the word of the Lord, that we which are alive and remain unto the coming of the Lord shall not prevent them which are asleep.* [16]*For the Lord himself shall descend from heaven with a*

shout, with the voice of the archangel, and with the trump of God: and the dead in Christ shall rise first:

In verse 15 above, it refers to '*we which are alive and remain*'. Paul is telling the saints in Thessalonica, the saints that go through the Tribulation will not all die, but some will remain alive at the end. They will not be raptured until the dead in Christ have been raptured. Let's look at the timing of the Rapture in Scripture.

(1Corinthians 15:52) [52]*In a moment, in the twinkling of an eye, at the last trump: for the trumpet shall sound, and the dead shall be raised incorruptible, and we shall be changed.*

When is that last trump? There are seven trumps in the end time prophecy. I believe the last trump referred to in 1Corinthians 15:52 is the seventh trump in the Book of the Revelation Chapter 11.

(Revelation 11:15) [15]*And the seventh angel sounded; and there were great voices in heaven, saying, The kingdoms of this world are become the kingdoms of our Lord, and of his Christ; and he shall reign for ever and ever.*

First, let's take a closer look at the last trump referred to in 1Corinthians 15:22 and the seventh trump in the Book of the Revelation.

(Revelation 10:7) [7]*But in the days of the voice of the seventh angel, when he shall begin to sound, the mystery of God should be finished, as he hath declared to his servants the prophets.*

(Matthew 24:36) [36]*But of that day and hour knoweth no man, no, not the angels of heaven, but my Father only.*

What is the mystery of God spoken of here? As far as I know, the only mystery of God is the Rapture. God has revealed everything else. Once again we need to look at 1Thessalonians 4.

> (1Thessalonians 4:14-16) 14*For if we believe that Jesus died and rose again, even so them also which sleep in Jesus will God bring with him.* 15*For this we say unto you by the word of the Lord, that we which are alive and remain unto the coming of the Lord shall not prevent them which are asleep.* 16*For the Lord himself shall descend from heaven with a shout, with the voice of the archangel, and with the trump of God: and the dead in Christ shall rise first:*

This Scripture clearly places the Rapture at the end of the Tribulation. It calls for the trump of God. The same trump as called for in 1Corinthians 15:52, which is the last trump.

I have a couple of points to make about the timing of the Rapture.

During the Tribulation there was '*a great multitude, which no man could number, of all nations, and kindreds, and people, and tongues*' (Revelation 7:9) of saints saved out of the Tribulation. If there was a Rapture of the saints prior to the Tribulation, where did this multitude come from? We know this multitude has to be more than 200,000,000 since John numbered the invading army at 200,000,000.

In the Book of the Revelation Chapter 13 the antichrist was granted to make war with the saints and to overcome them. If the saints were raptured before the Tribulation, why was the antichrist granted to make war with the saints that weren't there? His war with the saints will start at the beginning of the Great Tribulation.

(Revelation 13:5, 7) [5]*And there was given unto him a mouth speaking great things and blasphemies; and power was given unto him to continue forty and two months.* [7]*It was granted to him to make war with the saints and to overcome them. And authority was given him over every tribe, tongue, and nation.*

- The antichrist was given power over '*every tribe, tongue, and nation*'.
- The antichrist was given power '*to make war with the saints*'.
- The antichrist was given power '*to continue forty and two months*'.

These points make it clear the saints will be pursued by the antichrist all over the world for 42 months (3-1/2 years of 1260 days). This is what the Great Tribulation is about. It is about the worldwide torture and killing of the saints of Jesus Christ, those around the world with the Testimony of Jesus Christ.

Now that we know who gets raptured, let's look at how. What body will we have in Heaven? We can't get into Heaven without a spiritual body.

(1Corinthians 15:50) [50]*Now this I say, brethren, that flesh and blood cannot inherit the kingdom of God; neither doth corruption inherit incorruption*

(1Corinthians 15:44) [44]*It is sown a natural body; it is raised a spiritual body. There is a natural body, and there is a spiritual body*

So you ask, 'when will we get our spiritual body'? We will receive our spiritual body at the moment we are called to Heaven.

(1Corinthians 15:52-53) [52]*In a moment, in the twinkling of an eye, at the last trump: for the trumpet shall sound, and the dead shall be raised incorruptible, and we shall be changed.* [53]*For this corruptible must put on incorruption, and this mortal must put on immortality.*

For those that went directly from Earth to Heaven without dying, they must have received their spiritual body on the way to Heaven. Those that die during the Tribulation will receive their spiritual body when they die. They will not have to wait (sleep) for the Rapture to go to Heaven. Their souls will bypass the grave and proceed directly to Heaven.

(Revelation *7:9, 14)* [9]*After this I beheld, and, lo, a great multitude, which no man could number, of all nations, and kindreds, and people, and tongues, stood before the throne, and before the Lamb, clothed with white robes, and palms in their hands;* [14]*And I said unto him, Sir, thou knowest. And he said to me, These are they which came out of great tribulation, and have washed their robes, and made them white in the blood of the Lamb.*

This is a blessing the saints of the Tribulation receive the rest of us won't get. The rest of us will have to wait (sleep) in the grave until the Rapture.

(1Corinthians 15:51-54) [51]*Behold, I shew you a mystery; We shall not all sleep, but we shall all be changed,* [52]*In a moment, in the twinkling of an eye, at the last trump: for the trumpet shall sound, and the dead shall be raised incorruptible, and we shall be changed.* [53]*For this corruptible must put on incorruption, and this mortal must put on immortality.* [54]*So when this corruptible shall have put on incorruption, and this mortal shall have put on immortality, then shall be brought to pass the saying that is written, Death is swallowed up in victory.*

Those that have died in Christ before the Tribulation will be raised. They will 'sleep' until the time of the Rapture and then '*the dead shall rise first*'.

> (Revelation *20:6)* [6]*Blessed and holy is he that hath part in the first resurrection: on such the second death hath no power, but they shall be priests of God and of Christ, and shall reign with him a thousand years*

ANGEL OF THE GOSPEL BEING PREACHED

During the Tribulation Period, the Gospel will be preached. We have been told the Gospel will be preached to the entire world and then the end will come. This is accurate, but not the end they are talking about. The common interpretation of the end is the Rapture, which they claim comes before the Great Tribulation. The reality is the end referred to is actually the end of the Great Tribulation. The two witnesses and the saints will be raptured at the same time.

> (Revelation 14:6) [6]*And I saw another angel fly in the midst of heaven, having the everlasting gospel to preach unto them that dwell on the earth, and to every nation, and kindred, and tongue, and people,*

Here we are told the gospel will be preached during the Tribulation. Some believe this has to have been completed prior to the Tribulation. Does it? God will be sending two witnesses to earth to do just exactly that. Their sole purpose will be to testify of Jesus Christ during the Tribulation. With the advent of television and satellites, I'm sure they will be testifying around the world.

(Revelation 11:3) [3]*And I will give power unto my two witnesses, and they shall prophesy a thousand two hundred and threescore days, clothed in sackcloth.*

The two witnesses will be a spectacle and will be hated by most of the people on Earth and the people will rejoice when the antichrist kills them.

(Revelation 11:9-10) [9]*And they of the people and kindreds and tongues and nations shall see their dead bodies three days and an half, and shall not suffer their dead bodies to be put in graves.* [10]*And they that dwell upon the earth shall rejoice over them, and make merry, and shall send gifts one to another; because these two prophets tormented them that dwelt on the earth.*

The people of the earth will actually rejoice over their death.

(Matthew 24:14) [14]*And this gospel of the kingdom shall be preached in the entire world for a witness unto all nations; and then shall the end come.*

Here we are told is the 'end', the end of what? It is the end of God's patience with this world. Mankind has had their opportunity for salvation. Satan has had his opportunity to destroy the saints (the Great Tribulation). Now it's God's turn to take control. It is time for God to take vengeance on those that persecuted His people and to make the Earth a part of His kingdom.

The 'end' and the `start' of the Great Tribulation are not the same thing. The Great Tribulation comes before the 'end'.

In addition to the gospel continuing to be preached during the Tribulation period, the angel makes other proclamations.

PROCLAMATION OF JUDGMENT

(Revelation 14:6) [6]"*...Fear God and give glory to Him, for the hour of His judgment has come; and worship Him who made heaven and earth, the sea and springs of water.*"

He is proclaiming, "*Fear God for His judgment has come*". When is His judgment, or better, when does He meet out His judgment against those who have brought the abomination of desolation? He will bring judgment against those involved in the abomination of desolation at the end of the Tribulation and those that offend Him or do iniquity (violate God's laws).

(Matthew 13:41-43) [41]*The Son of man shall send forth his angels, and they shall gather out of his kingdom all things that offend, and them which do iniquity;* [42]*And shall cast them into a furnace of fire: there shall be wailing and gnashing of teeth.* [43]*Then shall the righteous shine forth as the sun in the kingdom of their Father.*

I think many miss the idea that the Tribulation is not of God. It is of Satan. We were given this example in the story of Job. God takes His turn after the Tribulation.

PROCLAMATION OF FALL OF BABYLON

(Revelation 14:8) [8]*and another angel followed, saying, "Babylon is fallen, is fallen, that great city, because she has made all nations drink of the wine of the wrath of her fornication.*"

The second proclamation deals with the fall of Babylon. Is he really talking about Babylon? The reference to Babylon includes "*that great city*". We have other references to the great city.

(Revelation 11:8) [8]"*And their bodies shall lie in the street of* *the great city*, *which spiritually is called Sodom and Egypt, where also our Lord was crucified.*"

Our Lord was not crucified in Babylon. He was crucified in Jerusalem. We can conclude when John refers to the great city, he is talking about Jerusalem. Also, the proclamation says Babylon (Jerusalem) is fallen. What does he mean by fallen? We can find the answer in the Book of the Revelation Chapter 18.

(Revelation 18:2) [2]*And he cried mightily with a loud voice, saying, "Babylon the great is fallen, is fallen, and has become a dwelling place of demons, a prison for every foul spirit, and a cage for every unclean and hated bird!"*

It has fallen from grace. The city has been taken over by darkness and every unclean and foul spirit. Here we have an indication of the "Abomination of Desolation."

(Daniel 11:31) [31]*And arms shall stand on his part, and they shall pollute the sanctuary of strength, and shall take away the daily sacrifice, and they shall place the abomination that maketh desolate.*

(Daniel 12:11) [11]*And from the time that the daily sacrifice shall be taken away, and the abomination that maketh desolate set up, there shall be a thousand two hundred and ninety days.*

In this Scripture, Daniel lets us know the sacrifice will be ended before the beginning of the Tribulation and the abomination that makes desolate is at the end of the Tribulation period. The Great Tribulation is 1260 days. The time between the sacrifice being taken away and the abomination being set up is 1290 days.

(Matthew 24:15-16) [15]*When ye therefore shall see the abomination of desolation, spoken of by Daniel the prophet, stand in the holy place, (whoso readeth, let him understand:)* [16]*Then let them which be in Judaea flee into the mountains:*

Danger! Danger! Danger! It's time to get as far away from Jerusalem as you can.

PROCLAMATION OF MARK OF THE BEAST

For those that go through the Tribulation, it is important for them to know about the mark of the beast. This is why this proclamation comes before the announcement of the Rapture!

If the saints allow themselves to receive the mark of the beast, they could be eternally damned. They may not go to Heaven and they may not go into eternity with God. The full study of the mark of the beast can be found in the chapter about the Beast and the False Prophet.

(Revelation 14:9-11) [9] *Then a third angel followed them, saying with a loud voice, "If anyone worships the beast and his image, and receives his mark on his forehead or on his hand,* [10] *he himself shall also drink of the wine of the wrath of God, which is poured out full strength into the cup of His indignation. He shall be tormented with fire and brimstone in the presence of the holy angels and in the presence of the Lamb.* [11] *And the smoke of their torment ascends forever and ever; and they have no rest day or night, who worship the beast and his image, and whoever receives the mark of his name."*

This proclamation is one that only those going through the Great Tribulation will have to deal with. It deals with the mark of the beast. This Scripture is a condensed version of the results for worshiping the beast and receiving the mark of the beast. It is not a pleasant outcome. If you want to be raptured, rule and reign with Christ in the Millennium, and go on into eternity with God; you better stay away from the worship of the beast and stay away from the mark of the beast.

In this condensed version it is easier to see the caveat provided. It says if you 'receive the mark and worship the beast' you will be tormented forever and ever. This indicates more than conceding to receive the mark. It indicates a belief in the deity of the beast. It indicates a willingness to worship the beast. For those that fall into this category there are some ominous warnings.

> (Revelation *14:9-10)* [9]*"If anyone worships the beast and his image, and receives his mark on his forehead or on his hand,* [10] *he himself shall also drink of the wine of the wrath of God,"*

> (Revelation 16:2) [2]*", so the first went and poured out his bowl upon the earth, and a foul and loathsome sore came upon the men who had the mark of the beast and those who worshiped his image.*

People could be forced to get the Mark of the Beast in prison or, in a hospital. Would this mean they are doomed? I think not. I can be made to receive the mark while unconscious; but I can't be forced to worship the beast.

In the Book of the Revelation 20:4, [4]*And I saw thrones, and they sat on them, and judgment was committed to them. Then I saw the souls of those who had been beheaded for their witness to Jesus and for the word of God, who had not worshiped the beast or his image, and had not received his mark on their foreheads or on their hands. And they lived and reigned with Christ for a thousand years".*

This Scripture is referring to the group, who had not worshiped the beast or his image, and had not received his mark on their foreheads or on their hands. This is the group I want to be in. They live and reign with Christ for a thousand years.

I don't want to mislead anyone. Those of us that do not go through the Great Tribulation are held to the same standard. In Exodus 20:3, "*Thou shalt have no other gods before me*". This is the first of the Ten Commandments and is born out again in verse 12 of the Book of the Revelation Chapter 14, "[12] *Here is the patience of the saints; here are those who keep the commandments of God and the faith of Jesus.* If you want to be counted with Christ, you better follow His commandments.

There is one more thing. The Scripture is a little vague on this; but I feel it is imperative I discus this further. If you receive the mark voluntarily to ease your way through, thinking you're just fooling the people of the antichrist; it could be disastrous. If you feign worshiping the beast for the same reason it could be disastrous. To make it through to the 'end', you have to maintain your testimony of Jesus Christ. We are to be a witness. Deception is a trait of Satan. Forewarned is forearmed.

PROCLAMATION FROM HEAVEN

(Revelation 14:*13)* [13]*Then I heard a voice from heaven saying to me, "Write: 'Blessed are the dead who die in the Lord from now on."*

This is referring to the saints that die during the Great Tribulation. As we have discussed previously, the saints that die during the Tribulation are allowed to go from Earth to Heaven directly. They do not have to suffer the grave and wait for the Rapture to get to Heaven. We saw the saints that died during the Great Tribulation in Heaven. The only other saints we saw in Heaven were the elders.

SUMMARY

We have seen the gospel being preached through the Tribulation. We have seen the pronouncement of the impending judgment. We have seen the Fall of Babylon (Jerusalem). We have seen the warning for those who might receive the mark of the beast. We have heard the proclamation from Heaven of the blessing for those that die after that point in time. These are all events leading up to the Reaping (Rapture) of the Earth. These events must all take place before the Rapture.

The gospel must be presented to the entire world right up to the moment of the Rapture to ensure all have an opportunity to receive it. The Rapture will come just before the impending wrath of God is unleashed upon the earth. The great city will have been overrun by the antichrist and his followers. Saints will have been tempted by the antichrist and the false prophet to receive the mark and worship the image of the antichrist. The saints that die in the Tribulation will receive a special blessing from God.

All of these things declared in Chapter 14:1-13 will come before the Rapture in Chapter 14:14-20. Now the proclamations are over. We are at one of the most blessed times in Scripture, the Reaping of the earth.

REAPING - THE RAPTURE

> (Revelation 14:*14-16)* [14]*Then I looked, and behold, a white cloud, and on the cloud sat One like the Son of Man, having on His head a golden crown, and in His hand a sharp sickle.* [15] *And another angel came out of the temple, crying with a loud voice to Him who sat on the cloud, "Thrust in Your sickle and reap, for the time has come for You to reap, for the harvest of the earth is ripe."* [16] *So He who sat on the cloud thrust in His sickle on the earth, and the earth was reaped.*

Glory, glory, this is what we are all waiting for. Jesus is coming for His saints. The harvest is ripe and ready to reap. Everyone has heard the gospel and made their choice.

(Revelation 14:*17)* [17]*Then another angel came out of the temple which is in heaven, he also having a sharp sickle.* Notice this is an angel; not, "One like the Son of Man, having on His head a golden crown, and in His hand a sharp sickle." This angel is not to reap the fruit as we will see in verse 18.

> (Revelation 14:*18)* [18]*And another angel came out from the altar, who had power over fire, and he cried with a loud cry to him who had the sharp sickle, saying, "Thrust in your sharp sickle and gather the clusters of the vine of the earth, for her grapes are fully ripe."*

Here again the angel is telling, "One like the Son of Man, having on His head a golden crown, and in His hand a sharp sickle," to reap the clusters of fruit. The harvest is ripe. Everyone destined to become believers will have become believers in Jesus Christ at that time.

There is another part of the crop yet to harvest, the chaff. The remnant left after the good fruit has been harvested.

(Revelation 14:19-20) [19]*So the angel thrust his sickle into the earth and gathered the vine of the earth, and threw it into the great winepress of the wrath of God.* [20] *And the winepress was trampled outside the city, and blood came out of the winepress, up to the horses' bridles, for one thousand six hundred furlongs.*

After the clusters (the fruit) are reaped, the vine of the earth (those invested in the earth) is reaped by another angel from the temple in Heaven. He also has a sharp sickle, and he reaps the vine of the earth and throws it into the winepress of the wrath of God.

Is this winepress of the wrath of God actually Armageddon? Let's take a quick look. Jesus gave us a very good sequence of events for this time in Matthew 24.

First...

(Matthew 24:29) [29]*Immediately after the tribulation of those days shall the sun be darkened, and the moon shall not give her light, and the stars shall fall from heaven, and the powers of the heavens shall be shaken:*

The next event after the end of the Tribulation of those days will be a series of natural disasters that cause the sun and moon to be darkened; the stars of the sky will fall and the powers of Heaven shall be shaken. This doesn't sound like Armageddon to me.

Second...

(Matthew 24:30-31) [30]*And then shall appear the sign of the Son of man in heaven: and then shall all the tribes of the earth mourn, and they shall see the Son of man coming in the clouds of heaven with power and great glory.* [31]*And he shall send his angels with a great sound of a trumpet, and they shall gather together his elect from the four winds, from one end of heaven to the other.*

This shows the return of the 'Son of man' with the armies of Heaven is after the period of natural disasters. That puts Armageddon after the time of natural disasters. This means the winepress of the wrath of God is not Armageddon. It is a time of the wrath of God brought in the form of bigger-than-ever natural disasters.

ABOMINATION OF DESOLATION

At the end of the Tribulation, there will be a final act of the antichrist and the false prophet that causes God to say enough. It will cause God to bring His wrath against the nations of the world for what they have done to His people. Before He brings His wrath upon the whole world, He will remove the remnant of His people in the Rapture.

What is the abomination that brings on the wrath of God? The act that causes God to bring His wrath is the abomination of desolation. We were first told of this in Daniel 12.

> (Dan 12:11-12) 11*And from the time that the daily sacrifice shall be taken away, and the abomination that maketh desolate set up, there shall be a thousand two hundred and ninety days.* 12*Blessed is he that waiteth, and cometh to the thousand three hundred and five and thirty days.*

As was mentioned earlier, after the end of the Great Tribulation there will be another period of time accounted for in Daniel 12 where he is told there are two time periods to come, 1290 days and 1335 days.

The first time period of 1290 days covers the Tribulation period plus an additional 30 days. Why the additional 30 days we are not told. I believe the extra thirty days are prior to the breaking of the treaty.

I believe and it's only a guess, the requiring that the sacrifices and oblations to be stopped, initiates a sequence of events that culminate in the breaking of the treaty. The end of the Tribulation period is fixed with the setting up of the abomination of desolation; it cannot be changed. The only answer is to add the 30 days before the beginning of the Tribulation.

Apparently, the sacrifices and oblations will be ended just before the breaking of the Seven-year treaty. It may even be what precipitates the breaking of the Treaty. If after 3-1/2 years the antichrist forces the then peaceful Jews from practicing their faith, they would most likely rebel.

At 1290 days from ending the sacrifices, the false prophet will have required the people of the earth to build an image (statue) of the antichrist. It will be placed in the Jewish Temple in Jerusalem at the end of the Great Tribulation. Oh, what a bad idea that will be.

> (Matthew 24:15) 15 *When ye therefore shall see the abomination of desolation, spoken of by Daniel the prophet, stand in the holy place, (whoso readeth, let him understand:)*

This is the 'abomination that maketh desolate' spoken of in Daniel. It is the setting up of the Image (Idol) of the antichrist and has it '*stand in the holy place*' in the Temple of God in Jerusalem. This abominable act will literally bring on desolation. Jesus warned the people of this in Matthew 24. God warned the Old Testament believers of the same thing in Zechariah 14:5. This abomination is referred to as the Abomination of Desolation because God finds this abomination so offensive He intends to hurl His wrath at the Earth and more specifically at Jerusalem and the seat of the beast. He has forewarned us of this event and encourages His people to abandon Jerusalem when they see this abomination. He is going to bring His wrath to bear for the next 45 days, which is 1335 days from the ending of the sacrifice. (1335 - 1290 = 45 days)

WRATH OF GOD

There are many that believe the saints are not to be in the Tribulation. They believe the saints are to be raptured before the time of the Tribulation. However, these same people don't believe the Tribulation and the wrath of God are two separate events. Let's take a look at what the Scriptures say.

> (Romans 5:9) [9]*Much more then, being now justified by his blood, we shall be saved from wrath through him.*
>
> (1Thessalonians 1:10) [10]*And to wait for his Son from heaven, whom he raised from the dead, even Jesus, which delivered us from the wrath to come.*
>
> (1Thessalonians 2:16)[16]*Forbidding us to speak to the Gentiles that they might be saved, to fill up their sins alway: for the wrath is come upon them to the uttermost.*
>
> (1Thessalonians 5:9) [9]*For God hath not appointed us to wrath, but to obtain salvation by our Lord Jesus Christ,*

Here we are told, '*we shall be saved from wrath through him,*' '*delivered us from the wrath to come.*' '*God hath not appointed us to wrath*'. These Scriptures do not refer to the Great Tribulation. They say the wrath. The wrath is God's wrath upon those filled up with their sins.

Whose wrath is he talking about? In the Book of the Revelation wrath is used 13 times. It is used once to refer to Satan when he is kicked out of Heaven and is come to Earth 'having great wrath'. The word wrath is used 12 times to refer to the wrath of God. The 16th Chapter of the Book of the Revelation is entirely devoted to the wrath of God.

> (Revelation 16:1) [1]*And I heard a great voice out of the temple saying to the seven angels, Go your ways, and pour out the bowls of the wrath of God upon the earth.*

Clearly, the saints are not intended to incur this wrath from God. The Tribulation is the wrath of Satan imposed against God's people, much like God allowed on Job. The wrath of God is a reciprocity upon those that came against His people.

This signals the start of the period referred to in Matthew 24:29 when '*the sun shall be darkened, and the moon shall not give her light, and the stars shall fall from heaven, and the powers of the heavens shall be shaken:*'

As we have seen, the saints will endure the Tribulation and those remaining at the end will be raptured and then there will be a time of trouble never before seen. Daniel tells us God shall deliver His people (Rapture) and then He will bring '*a time of trouble, such as never was since there was a nation even to that same time.*'

> (Daniel 12:1) [1]*And at that time shall Michael stand up, the great prince which standeth for the children of thy people: and there shall be a time of trouble, such as never was since there was a nation even to that same time: and at that time thy people shall be delivered, every one that shall be found written in the book.*

Daniel is told that Michael, the protector of Gods people, will stand up '*and at that time thy people shall be delivered, every one that shall be found written in the book.*'

John tells us in the Book of the Revelation Chapter 14 'another angel' (Michael) delivers the '*vine of the earth to the wine press of the wrath of God.*'

> (Revelation 14:17-19) [17]*And another angel came out of the temple which is in heaven, he also having a sharp sickle.* [18]*And another angel came out from the altar, which had power over fire; and cried with a loud cry to him that had the sharp sickle, saying, Thrust in thy sharp sickle, and gather the clusters of the vine of the earth; for her grapes are fully ripe.* [19]*And the angel thrust in his sickle into the earth, and gathered the vine of the earth, and cast it into the great winepress of the wrath of God.*

After the harvest of the ripe fruit, God delivers a judgment on the people of the earth that came against His people. The time of the wrath of God was told of by Jesus in Matthew 24:29. It places the time of God's wrath immediately after the tribulation of those days.

> (Matthew 24:29) [29]*Immediately after the tribulation of those days shall the sun be darkened, and the moon shall not give her light, and the stars shall fall from heaven, and the powers of the heavens shall be shaken:*

Jesus then schedules His return, when the whole world will see Him, after the time of God's wrath.

> (Matthew 24:30-31) [30]*And then shall appear the sign of the Son of man in heaven: and then shall all the tribes of the earth mourn, and they shall see the Son of man coming in the clouds of heaven with power and great glory.* [31]*And he shall send his angels with a great sound of a*

trumpet, and they shall gather together his elect from the four winds, from one end of heaven to the other.

(Revelation 19:14-15) [14]*And the armies which were in heaven followed him upon white horses, clothed in fine linen, white and clean.* [15]*And out of his mouth goeth a sharp sword, that with it he should smite the nations: and he shall rule them with a rod of iron: and he treadeth the winepress of the fierceness and wrath of Almighty God.*

This is not my schedule. This schedule was spoken by Jesus Christ and is reported in multiple places in the Bible. Jesus spoke of this in Matthew 24:29 and in Luke 21:25. It is alluded to in other places as well: Isaiah. 13:10; Joel 2:10; and Zephaniah 1:14-18. The reference in Zephaniah 1 gives us a little more clarification. It connects the wrath of God with the natural disasters. It tells us the wrath is against those that have sinned against the LORD.

(Zephaniah 1:14-18) [14]*The great day of the LORD is near, it is near, and hasteth greatly, even the voice of the day of the LORD: the mighty man shall cry there bitterly.* [15]*That day is a day of wrath, a day of trouble and distress, a day of wasteness and desolation, a day of darkness and gloominess, a day of clouds and thick darkness,* [16]*A day of the trumpet and alarm against the fenced cities, and against the high towers.* [17]*And I will bring distress upon men, that they shall walk like blind men, because they have sinned against the LORD: and their blood shall be poured out as dust, and their flesh as the dung.* [18]*Neither their silver nor their gold shall be able to deliver them in the day of the Lord's wrath; but the whole land shall be devoured by the fire of his jealousy: for he shall make even a speedy riddance of all them that dwell in the land.*

Zephaniah tells us there will be, '*even a speedy riddance of all them that dwell in the land.*' This is connected to the warning by God for all to leave Jerusalem when they see 'Abomination of Desolation' take place.

> (Matthew 24:15-21) [15]*When ye therefore shall see the abomination of desolation, spoken of by Daniel the prophet, stand in the holy place, (whoso readeth, let him understand:)* [16]*Then let them which be in Judaea flee into the mountains:* [17]*Let him which is on the housetop not come down to take any thing out of his house:* [18]*Neither let him which is in the field return back to take his clothes.* [19]*And woe unto them that are with child, and to them that give suck in those days!* [20]*But pray ye that your flight be not in the winter, neither on the Sabbath day:* [21]*For then shall be great tribulation, such as was not since the beginning of the world to this time, no, nor ever shall be.*

We have an abundance of Scriptures that let us know who is to receive the wrath of God, but Paul says it best in his letter to the Ephesians.

> (Ephesians 5:6) [6]*Let no man deceive you with vain words: for because of these things cometh the wrath of God upon the children of disobedience.*

This will happen after the saints have been raptured at the end of the Great Tribulation.

PLAGUES / NATURAL DISASTERS

Jesus gave us a warning of this period of His wrath when He said '*immediately after the tribulation the sun and the moon will be darkened, the stars shall fall from heaven, and the powers of the heavens shall be shaken:*' (Matthews

24:29). He told us He is going to use nature to create a time of trouble such as had never been seen. This could be called a second tribulation served up by God for those that came against His people. This tribulation appears to be God manipulating nature to bring His wrath against those that brought tribulation against His people.

Shortly after the two witnesses were resurrected (the same time as the Rapture), there was a great earthquake. It was so great; a tenth of the city (Jerusalem) was destroyed. This represents the beginning of His wrath. In the Book of the Revelation we have many accounts of natural disaster type events. I believe most, if not all of these occur during this 45-day period between the end of the 1290 days and the 1335th day. There are exceptions. They are trumpets 1 – 4, which occur before the Great Tribulation.

Some of the effects of these plagues will be:

- *Sores upon the men which had the mark of the beast, and upon them which worshiped his image* (Revelation 16:2).
- *Water to blood in the sea; and it became as the blood of a dead man: and every living soul died in the sea* (Revelation 16:3).
- *Water to blood in the rivers and fountains of waters; and they became blood* (Revelation 16:4).
- *Scorched with great heat, by the sun those that blasphemed God* (Revelation 16:8).
- *Darkness upon the seat of the beast; and his kingdom was full of darkness; and they gnawed their tongues for pain,* (Revelation 16:10).

- *Drought upon the great river Euphrates; and the water thereof was dried up, that the way of the kings of the east might be prepared* (Revelation 16:*12*).

This last plague is indeed the last plague. It allows the armies of the kings of the east to have a clear path to move into Israel and eventually to Armageddon. Following the wrath of God, comes Armageddon.

> (Matthew 24:30-31) [30]*And then shall appear the sign of the Son of man in heaven: and then shall all the tribes of the earth mourn, and they shall see the Son of man coming in the clouds of heaven with power and great glory.* [31]*And he shall send his angels with a great sound of a trumpet, and they shall gather together his elect from the four winds, from one end of heaven to the other.*

Armageddon is covered in the chapter titled Armageddon.

Chapter 10 SEQUENCE 5

BOWLS OF WRATH OF GOD

PREFACE

The Book of the Revelation 16:2-16

Now we move to the last of the commonly known sequences in the Book of the Revelation. It is known as the Bowls of the wrath of God poured out upon the earth. This is the first time we see the wrath of God used to describe a sequence of events that occurs before Armageddon. It is clearly after the Rapture. We saw in previous chapters, the saints are not to endure God's wrath.

> (Romans 5:9) [9]*Much more then, being now justified by his blood, we shall be saved from wrath through him.*
>
> (1Thessalonians 1:10) [10]*And to wait for his Son from heaven, whom he raised from the dead, even Jesus, which delivered us from the wrath to come.*
>
> (1Thessalonians 2:16) [16]*Forbidding us to speak to the Gentiles that they might be saved, to fill up their sins alway: for the* ***wrath*** *is come upon them to the uttermost.*
>
> (1Thessalonians *5:9)* [9]*For God hath not appointed us to wrath, but to obtain salvation by our Lord Jesus Christ,*

So who is to receive God's wrath?

(Ephesians 5:6) [6]*Let no man deceive you with vain words: for because of these things cometh the* ***wrath of God upon the children of disobedience.***

God's wrath here is meant for those that came against God's people and those that set up the image of the antichrist in the Temple of God.

TIME FRAME OF BOWLS

Some of these Bowls of Wrath seem to have a connection to other events we have already looked at. First, let's see if we can place a timetable for these Bowls of the wrath of God.

(Revelation 15:1) [1]*And I saw another sign in heaven, great and marvelous, seven angels having the seven last plagues; for in them is filled up the wrath of God.*

John tells us we are about to see the last seven plagues revealed to him by God. They are the wrath of God. In the next verse he gives the timing.

(Revelation 15:2) [2]*And I saw as it were a sea of glass mingled with fire: and them that had gotten the victory over the beast, and over his image, and over his mark, and over the number of his name, stand on the sea of glass, having the harps of God.*

John is seeing the saints that overcame during the Tribulation. In other words, the Tribulation is over; the Rapture has occurred. It is time for the wrath of God to be unleashed upon the Earth (Matthew 24:29). Now that we know when this takes place; let's see what takes place.

First Bowl: Loathsome Sores

(Revelation 16:2) [2]*So the first went and poured out his bowl upon the earth, and a foul and loathsome sore came upon the men who had the mark of the beast and those who worshiped his image.*

Is this related to the Locust attack in Chapter 9:4 of the Book of the Revelation?

(Revelation 9:4) [4]*They were commanded not to harm the grass of the earth, or any green thing, or any tree, but only those men who do not have the seal of God on their foreheads.*

Both of these plagues are against men only. No plants or other beings are to be infected. One does not affect men with the Mark of God on their forehead and the other affects only those with the Mark of the Beast. These could be the same event described differently, but they are not. The locust plague was before the Great Tribulation and this Bowl is after the Tribulation and is during the wrath of God which comes before Armageddon.

Second Bowl: The Sea Turns to Blood

(Revelation 16:3) [3]Then the second angel poured out his bowl on the sea, *and it became blood as of a dead man; and every living creature in the sea died.*

Is this related to the second trumpet in Chapter 8:8-9 of the Book of the Revelation?

Second Trumpet: The Seas Struck

(Revelation 8:8-9) [8] *Then the second angel sounded: And something like a great mountain burning with fire was thrown into the sea, and a*

Sixth Trumpet: The Angels from the Euphrates

(Revelation 9:13-21) [13] *Then the sixth angel sounded: And I heard a voice from the four horns of the golden altar which is before God,* [14] *saying to the sixth angel who had the trumpet, "Release the four angels who are bound at the great river Euphrates."* [15] *So the four angels, who had been prepared for the hour and day and month and year, were released to kill a third of mankind.* [16] *Now the number of the army of the horsemen was two hundred million; I heard the number of them.* [17] *And thus I saw the horses in the vision: those who sat on them had breastplates of fiery red, hyacinth blue, and sulfur yellow; and the heads of the horses were like the heads of lions; and out of their mouths came fire, smoke, and brimstone.* [18] *By these three plagues a third of mankind was killed—by the fire and the smoke and the brimstone which came out of their mouths.* [19] *For their power is in their mouth and in their tails; for their tails are like serpents, having heads; and with them they do harm.* [20] *But the rest of mankind, who were not killed by these plagues, did not repent of the works of their hands, that they should not worship demons, and idols of gold, silver, brass, stone, and wood, which can neither see nor hear nor walk.* [21] *And they did not repent of their murders or their sorceries or their sexual immorality or their thefts.*

This huge army (200,000,000) is coming against Israel and is allowed to complete the destruction Jerusalem.

(Revelation 17:16-18) [16]*"And the ten horns which thou sawest upon the beast, these shall hate the whore, and shall make her desolate and naked, and shall eat her flesh, and burn her with fire".* [17] *For, God has put it into their hearts to fulfill His purpose, to be of one mind, and to give their kingdom to the beast, until the words of God are fulfilled.* [18] *And the third of the sea became blood. [9] And a third of the living creatures in the sea died, and a third of the ships were destroyed.*

Even though both of these affect the sea they do it differently. The second trumpet affected a third of the sea and a third of the creatures in the sea died. The third bowl affected the entire sea and every creature in the sea died. This is a much more tragic event.

Next we move to the rivers and springs contaminated.

Third Bowl: The Waters Turn to Blood.

(Revelation 16:4-7) [4] *Then the third angel poured out his bowl on the rivers and springs of water, and they became blood.* [5] *And I heard the angel of the waters saying: "You are righteous, O Lord, The One who is and who was and who is to be, Because You have judged these things.* [6] *For, they have shed the blood of saints and prophets, And You have given them blood to drink. For it is their just due."*[7] *And I heard another from the altar saying, "Even so, Lord God Almighty, true and righteous are Your judgments."*

Compare this to the third trumpet.

Third Trumpet: The Waters Struck

(Revelation 8:10-11) [10] *Then the third angel sounded: And a great star fell from heaven, burning like a torch, and it fell on a third of the rivers and on the springs of water.* [11]*The name of the star is Wormwood. A third of the waters became wormwood, and many men died from the water, because it was made bitter.*

Here again these events are similar but not the same. The trumpet affects a third of the waters and the bowl appears to affect all the rivers and springs.

Fourth Bowl: Men Are Scorched

> (Revelation 16:8-9) [8]*Then the fourth angel poured out his bowl on the sun, and power was given to him to scorch men with fire.* [9]*And men were scorched with great heat, and they blasphemed the name of God who has power over these plagues; and they did not repent and give Him glory.*

This bowl seems to affect the intensity of the sun's radiation, possibly a solar flare. Unlike the first three bowls of wrath of God, this one appears to affect the entire world. It would seem anything associated with the sun would have an impact on other parts of the world as well. If it only lasted an hour, it would still affect all lands north and south of Israel. This opens the door to those who speculate that the Tribulation plagues are in fact a worldwide event.

This next Bowl is specifically focused at Jerusalem. It is on the throne of the beast.

Fifth Bowl: Darkness and Pain

> (Revelation 16:10-11) [10] *Then the fifth angel poured out his bowl on the throne of the beast, and his kingdom became full of darkness; and they gnawed their tongues because of the pain.* [11] *They blasphemed the God of heaven because of their pains and their sores, and did not repent of their deeds.*

What is poured out on the throne of the beast? His kingdom is a kingdom of darkness. Does this mean the darkness is allowed to totally consume the kingdom of the antichrist? You can count on it. They are feeling the full effect of the wrath of God.

This next Bowl is clearly the last step before Armageddon.

Sixth Bowl: Euphrates Dried Up

> (Revelation 16:12) [12]*Then the sixth angel poured out his bowl on the great river Euphrates, and its water was dried up, so that the way of the kings from the east might be prepared.*

There are a couple of possibilities of how this will be accomplished. It could be the result of drought or it could be manmade. In Turkey there are a series of dams installed on the Euphrates River and its tributaries. The dams were installed in the 1990s. These are being used to irrigate fields in central Turkey. If there were to be a drought and Turkey kept water for their irrigation projects, the Euphrates could very well be dried up. Or, the Turks could just shut off the water for a period of time by holding the water in their lakes by means of raising the spillways and allowing the armies to pass through.

> (Revelation 16:13-16) [13]*And I saw three unclean spirits like frogs coming out of the mouth of the dragon, out of the mouth of the beast, and out of the mouth of the false prophet.* [14] *For they are spirits of demons, performing signs, which go out to the kings of the earth and of the whole world, to gather them to the battle of that great day of God Almighty.* [15] *Behold, I am coming as a thief. Blessed is he who watches, and keeps his garments, lest he walk naked and they see his shame.* [16] *And they gathered them together to the place called in Hebrew, Armageddon."*

This is clearly tied to the event in the Book of the Revelation 9:13-21, the Sixth Trumpet. The 200,000,000-man army is unleashed on Israel.

woman whom you saw is that great city which reigns over the kings of the earth."

. In the Book of the Revelation 18:2 we are told why God has judged Israel (Jerusalem) so harshly.

(Revelation 18:2) [2]*"And he cried mightily with a strong voice saying, Babylon the great is fallen, is fallen, and is become the habitation devils, and the hold of every foul spirit, and the cage of every unclean and hateful bird".*

In the Book of the Revelation 17:18; 18:2, John refers to 'that great city' and to 'Babylon the great'. Is he really talking about Babylon? No, he is talking about Jerusalem. In the Book of the Revelation 11:8, where he is talking about the two witnesses he says, *"And their bodies shall lie in the street of the great city, which spiritually is called Sodom and Egypt, where also our Lord was crucified."* Where was Jesus crucified? It certainly wasn't the city of Babylon. This tells us when John refers to the great city, he is talking about Jerusalem.

That great city has fallen from grace. The city has been taken over by darkness and every unclean and foul spirits. This is a notification of the "Abomination of Desolation." God has brought this judgment against her because she has turned from Him. Once this destruction is over, it's time for Armageddon.

Seventh Bowl – It is done

(Revelation 16:17) [17]*And the seventh angel poured out his bowl into the air; and there came a great voice out of the temple of heaven, from the throne, saying, It is done.*

From here it's on to the Millennium. That concludes our study of the Seven Bowls, the fifth sequence to Armageddon.

Chapter 11 Sequence 6 – The Final Path

The Book of the Revelation 19:1-21

ARMY FROM HEAVEN

Now we are at the last of the sequences leading to Armageddon. It is found in the Book of the Revelation 19:1-21.

> (Revelation 19:1-5) [1]*After these things, I heard a loud voice of a great multitude in heaven, saying, "Alleluia! Salvation and glory and honor and power belong to the Lord our God!* [2] *For true and righteous are His judgments, because He has judged the great harlot who corrupted the earth with her fornication; and He has avenged on her the blood of His servants shed by her."* [3] *Again they said, "Alleluia! Her smoke rises up forever and ever!"* [4] *And the twenty-four elders and the four living creatures fell down and worshiped God who sat on the throne, saying, "Amen! Alleluia!"* [5] *Then a voice came from the throne, saying, "Praise our God, all you His servants and those who fear Him, both small and great!"*

Here we have another reference to an event that happened elsewhere in the Book of the Revelation. Let's work backwards on this one.

A GREAT MULTITUDE IN HEAVEN

This sequence opens with a great multitude in Heaven. Who are these people? In the Book of the Revelation 7:9, 13, 14, we are told who they are.

(Revelation 7:9-10) [9]*After these things I looked, and behold, a great multitude which no one could number, of all nations, tribes, peoples, and tongues, standing before the throne and before the Lamb, clothed with white robes, with palm branches in their hands,* [10] *and crying out with a loud voice, saying, "Salvation belongs to our God who sits on the throne, and to the Lamb!"*

(Revelation 7:13-14) [13] *Then one of the elders answered, saying to me, "Who are these arrayed in white robes, and where did they come from?"* [14] *And I said to him, "Sir, you know." So he said to me, "These are the ones who come out of the great tribulation, and washed their robes and made them white in the blood of the Lamb.*

This multitude is made up of saints killed during the Great Tribulation, the 24 elders, and those saints raptured. The raptured saints are those that died before the Tribulation and those saints still alive on earth at the end of the Tribulation.

WHO IS THE GREAT HARLOT?

In the Book of the Revelation Chapter 17 we have a description of the great harlot. She sits on many waters. She is referred to as the woman, the harlot, Babylon the Great, the Mother of Harlots and Abominations of the Earth. In the final verse of the chapter we are told the woman is "that great city which reigneth over the kings of the earth". Remember at the time this happens the beast and the false prophet are ruling the whole earth from Jerusalem. In the Book of the Revelation 11:8 talking about the two witnesses we are told, "*And their bodies shall lie in the street of the great city, which spiritually is called Sodom and Egypt, where also our Lord was crucified.*" Where was Jesus crucified? It certainly wasn't the city of Babylon. This tells us when John refers to the great city, he is talking about Jerusalem.

God will use His enemies to bring His judgment against Jerusalem.

> (Revelation 17:16-18) [16]*And the ten horns which you saw on the beast, these will hate the harlot, make her desolate and naked, eat her flesh and burn her with fire.* [17]*For God has put it into their hearts to fulfill His purpose, to be of one mind, and to give their kingdom to the beast, until the words of God are fulfilled.* [18]*And the woman whom you saw is that great city which reigns over the kings of the earth.*"

The beast of the fourth empire will be made up of ten nations. These ten nations are referred to here as ten horns. God will use the ten horns that will have given over their authority to the beast (antichrist); and put it in their mind to fulfill his purpose to fulfill his judgment, to make the great city desolate, to make her naked and burn her with fire. He is going to put it in their minds to come against Jerusalem with an army of 200,000,000.

KINGS OF THE EAST CROSS THE EUPHRATES

In the Book of the Revelation Chapters 9 and 16, we have accommodation made to get the 200,000,000-man army across the Euphrates River.

> (Revelation 16:12) [12]"*Then the sixth angel poured out his bowl on the great river Euphrates, and its water was dried up, so that the way of the kings from the east might be prepared.*

First, the Euphrates River will be dried up. This may be done by drought or it may be manmade by using the irrigation water dams in

Turkey to hold back the water. Then the four rulers of the armies of the east are given the attack command.

> (Revelation *9:13-18)* [13]*Then the sixth angel sounded: And I heard a voice from the four horns of the golden altar which is before God,* [14] *saying to the sixth angel who had the trumpet, "Release the four angels who are bound at the great river Euphrates."* [15] *So the four angels, who had been prepared for the hour and day and month and year, were released to kill a third of mankind.* [16] *Now the number of the army of the horsemen was two hundred million; I heard the number of them.* [17] *And thus I saw the horses in the vision: those who sat on them had breastplates of fiery red, hyacinth blue, and sulfur yellow; and the heads of the horses were like the heads of lions; and out of their mouths came fire, smoke, and brimstone.* [18] *By these three plagues a third of mankind was killed—by the fire and the smoke and the brimstone which came out of their mouths.*

Now we see the connection of the drying up of the Euphrates River to allow the 200,000,000-man army to cross. We see the army is prepared for an hour, day, month, and year. Prepared by whom? Prepared by God. Then we see the degree of conflict, in that a third of mankind will be killed. It doesn't appear we are told of everyone involved. If you add the 200,000,000 to the entire population of Israel, it won't add up to the one-third of mankind. It appears the 1/3 of mankind to be killed is actually 1/3 of mankind in Israel.

> (Revelation 19:6-8) [6]*And I heard, as it were, the voice of a great multitude, as the sound of many waters and as the sound of mighty thunderings, saying, "Alleluia! For the Lord God Omnipotent reigns!* [7] *Let us be glad and rejoice and give Him glory, for the marriage of the Lamb has come, and His wife has made herself ready."* [8] *And to her it was*

granted to be arrayed in fine linen, clean and bright, for the fine linen is the righteous acts of the saints.

Here is another reference to the multitude in Heaven worshiping God and they are being prepared for the marriage supper of the lamb. They are simply waiting for the victory over Satan and his minions.

(Revelation 19:9-10) [9]*Then he said to me, "Write: 'Blessed are those who are called to the marriage supper of the Lamb!'" And he said to me, "These are the true sayings of God."* [10] *And I fell at his feet to worship him. But he said to me, "See that you do not do that! I am your fellow servant, and of your brethren who have the testimony of Jesus. Worship God! For the testimony of Jesus is the spirit of prophecy."*

Blessed are those called to the Marriage Supper of the Lamb. Wow, who wouldn't want to be in that group? And we are told, "*the testimony of Jesus is the spirit of prophecy.*" You won't get to spend eternity with God without it.

HERE HE COMES

In the Book of the Revelation 19:11-21, we see the most complete coverage of Armageddon.

(Revelation 19:11-16) [11] *Now I saw heaven opened, and behold, a white horse. And He who sat on him was called Faithful and True, and in righteousness He judges and makes war.* [12] *His eyes were like a flame of fire, and on His head were many crowns. He had a name written that no one knew except Himself.* [13] *He was clothed with a robe dipped in blood, and His name is called The Word of God.* [14] *And the armies in heaven, clothed in fine linen, white and clean, followed Him on white horses.* [15]

Now out of His mouth goes a sharp sword, that with it He should strike the nations. And He Himself will rule them with a rod of iron. He Himself treads the winepress of the fierceness and wrath of Almighty God. [16] *And He has on His robe and on His thigh a name written: KING OF KINGS AND LORD OF LORDS.*

What a sight, Jesus on a white horse, His eyes like a flame of fire, crowns on His head, clothed in a robe dipped in blood, and the armies of Heaven clothed in white linen following Him, also on white horses. The name on His robe is, "*KING OF KINGS AND LORD OF LORDS*".

He is the one that treads the winepress of the fierceness and wrath of Almighty God. He is wrapping up the end of His wrath. This concludes the sixth sequence to Armageddon. The next chapter will cover Armageddon

Chapter 12 ARMAGEDDON

PREFACE

After God has brought His wrath against those that came against His people; it is time for Jesus to return with the armies of Heaven to meet out judgment at Armageddon.

> (Matthew 24:30-31) [30]*And then shall appear the sign of the Son of man in heaven: and then shall all the tribes of the earth mourn, and they shall see the Son of man coming in the clouds of heaven with power and great glory.* [31]*And he shall send his angels with a great sound of a trumpet, and they shall gather together his elect from the four winds, from one end of heaven to the other.*

> (Revelation 19:14-15) [14]*And the armies which were in heaven followed him upon white horses, clothed in fine linen, white and clean.* [15]*And out of his mouth goeth a sharp sword, that with it he should smite the nations: and he shall rule them with a rod of iron: and he treadeth the winepress of the fierceness and wrath of Almighty God.*

ARMAGEDDON

Armageddon will be the armies of the antichrist coming against Israel in the valley of Megiddo. This will be a big problem for them. God is going to meet them there and the result is not good for the antichrist, the false prophet and their followers.

We have looked at six separate sequences leading to Armageddon. Let's combine them here.

BOOK OF SEALS - SIXTH SEAL

(Revelation 6:12-17) [12]*And I beheld when he had opened the sixth seal, and, lo, there was a great earthquake; and the sun became black as sackcloth of hair, and the moon became as blood;* [13]*And the stars of heaven fell unto the earth, even as a fig tree casteth her untimely figs, when she is shaken of a mighty wind.* [14]*And the heaven departed as a scroll when it is rolled together; and every mountain and island were moved out of their places.* [15]*And the kings of the earth, and the great men, and the rich men, and the chief captains, and the mighty men, and every bondman, and every free man, hid themselves in the dens and in the rocks of the mountains;* [16]*And said to the mountains and rocks, Fall on us, and hide us from the face of him that sitteth on the throne, and from the wrath of the Lamb:* [17]*For the great day of his wrath is come; and who shall be able to stand*

TRUMPETS - SIXTH TRUMPET

(Revelation 19:14-16) [14] *Saying to the sixth angel which had the trumpet, Loose the four angels which are bound in the great river Euphrates.* [15]*And the four angels were loosed, which were prepared for an hour, and a day, and a month, and a year, for to slay the third part of men.* [16]*And the number of the army of the horsemen were two hundred thousand thousand: and I heard the number of them.*

TWO WITNESSES - AFTER THE WITNESSES ARE RESURRECTED

(Revelation 11:13-14) [13]*And the same hour was there a great earthquake, and the tenth part of the city fell, and in the earthquake were slain of men seven thousand: and the remnant were affrighted, and gave glory to the God of heaven.* [14]*The second woe is past; and, behold, the third woe cometh quickly.*

RAPTURE - AFTER THE SAINTS GO TO HEAVEN

(Revelation 14:19-20) [19]*And the angel thrust in his sickle into the earth, and gathered the vine of the earth, and cast it into the great winepress of the wrath of God.* [20]*And the winepress was trodden without the city, and blood came out of the winepress, even unto the horse bridles, by the space of a thousand and six hundred furlongs.*

BOWLS OF WRATH OF GOD - SIXTH BOWL

(Revelation 16:12-16) [12]*And the sixth angel poured out his bowl upon the great river Euphrates; and the water thereof was dried up, that the way of the kings of the east might be prepared.* [13]*And I saw three unclean spirits like frogs come out of the mouth of the dragon, and out of the mouth of the beast, and out of the mouth of the false prophet.* [14]*For they are the spirits of devils, working miracles, which go forth unto the kings of the earth and of the whole world, to gather them to the battle of that great day of God Almighty.* [15]*Behold, I come as a thief. Blessed is he that watcheth, and keepeth his garments, lest he walk naked, and they see his shame. [16] And he gathered them together into a place called in the Hebrew tongue Armageddon.*

ARMY FROM HEAVEN - HERE HE COMES

(Revelation 19:14-18) *[14] And the armies which were in heaven followed him upon white horses, clothed in fine linen, white and clean. [15] And out of his mouth goeth a sharp sword, that with it he should smite the nations: and he shall rule them with a rod of iron: and he treadeth the winepress of the fierceness and wrath of Almighty God. [16] And he hath on his vesture and on his thigh a name written, KING OF KINGS, AND LORD OF LORDS. [17] And I saw an angel standing in the sun; and he cried with a loud voice, saying to all the fowls that fly in the midst of heaven, Come and gather yourselves together unto the supper of the great God; [18] That ye may eat the flesh of kings, and the flesh of captains, and the flesh of mighty men, and the flesh of horses, and of them that sit on them, and the flesh of all men, both free and bond, both small and great.*

All of these events happen before Armageddon. Some will occur at the same times as others. Some will be sequential.

SUMMARY

During the Great Tribulation, God will place His two witnesses on the earth to testify of salvation through Jesus Christ. They will be on earth testifying during the entire Tribulation. At the end of the Tribulation period the beast (antichrist) will slay them. They will lay in the street for three days and then God will restore them and call them back to Heaven. At that time there will be a great earthquake, seven thousand men will die, and a tenth of the city will collapse.

At the same time the two witnesses are resurrected, I believe the Rapture will occur. The Rapture cannot occur until God decides all of the saints that are to be killed during the Tribulation are killed. At that time God will remove (Rapture) all of the remaining saints from the earth. At the end of the Rapture, the vine of the earth will be reaped and cast into the *winepress of the wrath of God.* This wrath of God, I believe is the period Jesus spoke of. Jesus told His disciples in Matthew 24;

> (Matthew 24:29) [29]*Immediately after the tribulation of those days shall the sun be darkened, and the moon shall not give her light, and the stars shall fall from heaven, and the powers of the heavens shall be shaken:*

Our next sequence is the realization of Jesus' prophecy. When the sixth seal is opened in the Book of the Revelation Chapter 6, we are told virtually the same thing is happening as was predicted in Matthew 24:29.

> (Revelation 6:12-13) [12]*And I beheld when he had opened the sixth seal, and, lo, there was a great earthquake; and the sun became black as sackcloth of hair, and the moon became as blood;* [13]*And the stars of heaven fell unto the earth*

This begins a period of unbelievable disasters brought by God upon those that persecuted His people or allowed the persecution of His people.

TIME REFRESHER

Before we proceed to the next event I need to do a little refresher of the times of the Tribulation. We have four time periods mentioned that pertain to the Great Tribulation and wrath of God periods.

- Seven years, 1260 days(42 months – 3-1/2 years) , 1290 days, and 1335 days.
- Seven years is the original length of the treaty negotiated between the antichrist and Israel.
- Twelve-hundred sixty days is the accepted length of the Tribulation period. This is the time the antichrist will be given to do his thing. It is the amount of time the two witnesses will have to testify to the whole world.
- Twelve-hundred ninety days (Daniel *12:11)* gives us another thirty days to account for. We don't have an explanation for the additional thirty days added by Daniel.

(Daniel *9:27)* 27*And he shall confirm the covenant with many for one week: and in the midst of the week he shall cause the sacrifice and the oblation to cease.*

The Scripture doesn't say the cancellation of the sacrifices and oblations is at the same time as the breaking of the treaty. It could be that stopping the sacrifices and oblations are the trigger that causes the events to take place, that cause or allow the antichrist to break the treaty. We know the end of the Tribulation is not going to change. Here again we don't have enough information to know for sure.

I believe but can't prove the antichrist or false prophet will order the sacrifices and oblations to be ended 30 days before the mid-point of the Seven-year treaty. That would be 1290 days before the end of the Great Tribulation.

Daniel gave us another number of days to figure out, 1335(Daniel *12:12*). That gives us another 45 days to account for. If the ending of the sacrifice and oblation is 30 days before the treaty is broken, then we have 45 days added after the end of the Tribulation. Let's look at a timeline to try to get a clearer understanding of the relationship of these times.

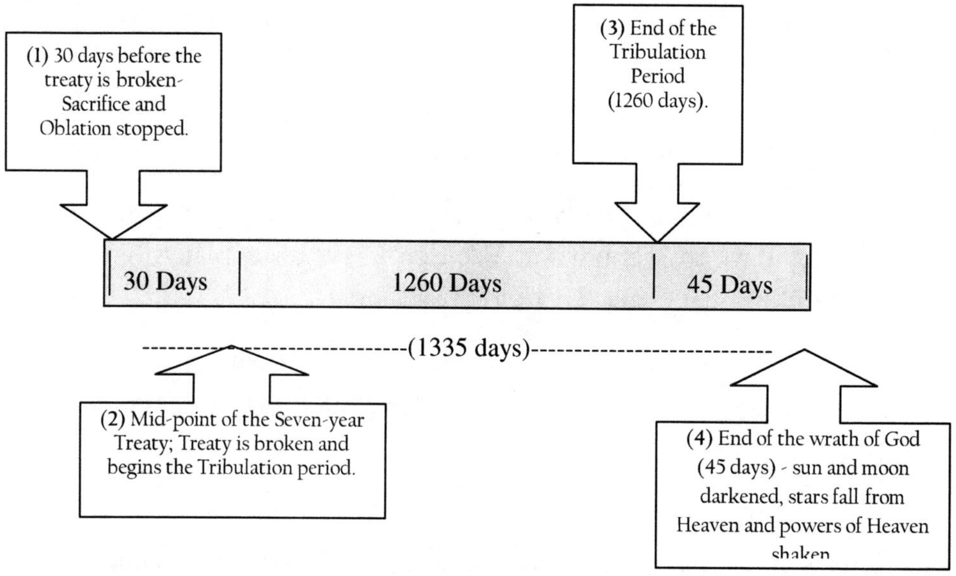
(1) 30 days before the treaty is broken- Sacrifice and Oblation stopped.
(3) End of the Tribulation Period (1260 days).
30 Days
1260 Days
45 Days
(1335 days)
(2) Mid-point of the Seven-year Treaty; Treaty is broken and begins the Tribulation period.
(4) End of the wrath of God (45 days) - sun and moon darkened, stars fall from Heaven and powers of Heaven shaken

In the middle, between (2) and (3) we have the Tribulation Period (1260 days). To the left between (1) and (2) we have the 30 days before the Tribulation starts. This is my guess, not based on Scripture. To the right between (3) and (4) we have the extra 45 days. This is my guess, not based on Scripture.

The 30 days before the Tribulation is difficult to determine accurately. However, the 45 days after is called out in Matthew 24, but it isn't given a period of time.

(Matthew 24:29) [29]*Immediately after the tribulation of those days shall the sun be darkened, and the moon shall not give her light, and the stars shall fall from heaven, and the powers of the heavens shall be shaken:*

This will be the time of God's wrath, (Revelation 16:1) [1]*Go your ways, and pour out the bowls of the wrath of God upon the earth.*. This is the event God is going to protect us from. I believe the saints will be raptured just before this time of God's wrath. The following Scriptures show we are exempted from the wrath of God. We are not exempted from tribulation.

(Roman 5:9) [9] *Much more then, being now justified by his blood, we shall be saved from wrath through him.*

(Ephesians 5:6) [6]*Let no man deceive you with vain words: for because of these things cometh the wrath of God upon the children of disobedience.*

(1Thessalonians 1:10) [10]*And to wait for his Son from heaven, whom he raised from the dead, even Jesus, which delivered us from the wrath to come.*

(1Thessalonians 5:9) [9]*For God hath not appointed us to wrath, but to obtain salvation by our Lord Jesus Christ,*

Near the end of the forty-five days of God's wrath comes the sixth bowl which dries up the Euphrates River preparing the way for the kings of the east.

The sixth bowl is followed almost immediately by the sixth trumpet. The sixth trumpet releases four angels (presumably representing four nations). These four angels are going to be prepared for the hour, day, month and year to slay a third part of men. They will have an army of 200,000,000 men.

We are told the Euphrates is dried up to make way for the kings of the east and they are headed to Armageddon; but before they get to Armageddon they are to kill 1/3 of mankind. Is that 1/3 of the entire earth, or is it 1/3 of mankind in Israel?

On Oct 21, 2009, the world population was 6,791,903,951. One-third of the world population would be 2,263,967,984. Do you think a 200,000,000-man army could kill over 2 billion people, possible, but isn't likely? The population of Israel was 7,411,000. A third of Israel's population would be 2,470,333. This would be a huge blood bath; but not as large as the 200,000,000 God will destroy at Armageddon.

ARMAGEDDON - THE GOOD GUYS SHOW UP

Heaven will open and Jesus will appear followed by the armies from Heaven. They will all be clothed in white linen. Jesus has a vest with King of Kings and Lord of Lords written on it. All the fowls that fly in the midst of Heaven will be gathered to eat the flesh of kings, and captains, and mighty men, and the flesh of horses, and of them that sit on them, and the flesh of all men, both free and bond, both small and great.

> (Revelation 19:11-18) [11]*And I saw heaven opened, and behold a white horse; and he that sat upon him was called Faithful and True, and in righteousness he doth judge and make war.* [12]*His eyes were as a flame of*

fire, and on his head were many crowns; and he had a name written, that no man knew, but he himself. [13]*And he was clothed with a vesture dipped in blood: and his name is called The Word of God.* [14]*And the armies which were in heaven followed him upon white horses, clothed in fine linen, white and clean.* [15]*And out of his mouth goeth a sharp sword, that with it he should smite the nations: and he shall rule them with a rod of iron: and he treadeth the winepress of the fierceness and wrath of Almighty God.* [16]*And he hath on his vesture and on his thigh a name written, KING OF KINGS, AND LORD OF LORDS.* [17]*And I saw an angel standing in the sun; and he cried with a loud voice, saying to all the fowls that fly in the midst of heaven, Come and gather yourselves together unto the supper of the great God;* [18]*That ye may eat the flesh of kings, and the flesh of captains, and the flesh of mighty men, and the flesh of horses, and of them that sit on them, and the flesh of all men, both free and bond, both small and great.*

ARMAGEDDON: ONE-SIDED

They call it the battle at Armageddon. I don't know why they would call it a battle. It's a bit one-sided. Satan, the antichrist, and the false prophet bring their armies against Jesus Christ and the armies of Heaven. Believe me; Jesus Christ isn't coming as a peacemaker. He is coming bent on the destruction of the enemies of His people.

(Revelation 19:19-21) [19]*And I saw the beast, and the kings of the earth, and their armies, gathered together to make war against him that sat on the horse, and against his army.* [20]*And the beast was taken, and with him the false prophet that wrought miracles before him, with which he deceived them that had received the mark of the beast, and them that worshipped his image. These both were cast alive into a lake of fire burning with brimstone. [21]And the remnant were slain with the sword of him that sat upon the horse, which sword proceeded out of his mouth: and all the fowls were filled with their flesh.*

The battle of Armageddon begins with the beast and false prophet being cast alive into the lake of fire burning with brimstone. Not only are the beast and the false prophet destroyed, but their armies, as well. What isn't said here is their nations are not destroyed. This is an often-missed point. We will see at the end of the Millennium, these nations will come into play again. We also need to note the destruction of the antichrist (the beast). This answers the question of whether or not the antichrist is Satan incarnate. Satan's fate is yet to be told.

SATAN'S END

Satan's fate is different from the beast (antichrist) and the false prophet. Satan is taken after Armageddon and placed in the bottomless pit and isn't let out to deceive again until the end of the Millennium.

(Revelation 20:2-3) *[2]And he laid hold on the dragon, that old serpent, which is the Devil, and Satan, and bound him a thousand years, [3]And cast him into the bottomless pit, and shut him up, and set a seal upon him, that he should deceive the nations no more, till the thousand years should be fulfilled: and after that he must be loosed a little season.*

Satan is to be bound in the bottomless pit where he had released the beast and the plague of locusts. He will be there for virtually the entire Millennium.

(Revelation 11:*15-17)* [15]*And the seventh angel sounded; and there were great voices in heaven, saying, 'the kingdoms of this world are become the kingdoms of our Lord, and of his Christ; and he shall reign for ever and ever'.* [16]*And the four and twenty elders, which sat before God on their seats, fell upon their faces, and worshipped God,* [17]*Saying, 'We give thee thanks, O LORD God Almighty, which art, and wast, and art to come; because thou hast taken to thee thy great power, and hast reigned'.*

The world will never be the same. Christ has taken direct charge over the Earth and stays on Earth through the Millennium. This concludes our study of Armageddon.

Chapter 13 MILLENNIUM THROUGH ETERNITY

ARMAGEDDON

Just prior to the Millennium we have Armageddon. Armageddon is the destruction of the armies of the beast and the beast (antichrist) along with the false prophet are cast into the lake of fire.

> (Revelation 19:19-21) 19 *And I saw the beast, and the kings of the earth, and their armies, gathered together to make war against him that sat on the horse, and against his army.* 20 *And the beast was taken, and with him the false prophet that wrought miracles before him, with which he deceived them that had received the mark of the beast, and them that worshipped his image. These both were cast alive into a lake of fire burning with brimstone.* 21 *And the remnant were slain with the sword of him that sat upon the horse, which sword proceeded out of his mouth: and all the fowls were filled with their flesh.*

WHO GETS INTO THE MILLENNIUM

Did anyone ever talk to you about the nations left around the world throughout the Millennium? I don't believe I ever heard anyone talk about these nations. There will be nations that live on through the Millennium. We know they are there two ways. One, there is no mention of them being destroyed or eliminated. Second, we know they are there because they are there at the end of the Millennium for Satan to go out and deceive.

(Revelation 20:8) [8]*And shall go out to deceive the nations which are in the four quarters of the earth, Gog, and Magog, to gather them together to battle: the number of whom is as the sand of the sea.*

If they are Christian nations, how would Satan be able to deceive them? Satan will go out and deceive them (Gog and Magog) into coming against God one more time.

SAINTS IN THE MILLENNIUM

(Revelation 20:4) [4]*And I saw thrones, and they sat upon them, and judgment was given unto them: and I saw the souls of them that were beheaded for the witness of Jesus, and for the word of God, and which had not worshipped the beast, neither his image, neither had received his mark upon their foreheads, or in their hands; and they lived and reigned with Christ a thousand years.*

The saints that have overcome the earth will move on to the Millennium to rule and reign. Who are these saints? They will include the elders (from Old and New Testament times) and saints killed during the Tribulation. Then we have the Rapture group, those saints alive at the end of the Tribulation, and the dead in Christ from before the Tribulation. Now you are going to read something I had never heard discussed before I started this study.

REIGN OVER WHO?

After Armageddon, John sees thrones and those that sat upon them were given the power of judgment. Who do you suppose is given the power of judgment and who are they given judgment over?

(Revelation 20:4) [4]*And I saw thrones, and they sat on them, and judgment was committed to them. Then I saw the souls of those who had been beheaded for their witness to Jesus and for the word of God, who had not worshiped the beast or his image, and had not received his mark on their foreheads or on their hands. And they lived and reigned with Christ for a thousand years".*

The answer as to who they are comes in the next verse.

(Revelation *20:5-6)* [5]*But the rest of the dead lived not again until the thousand years were finished. This is the first resurrection.* [6]*Blessed and holy is he that hath part in the first resurrection (Rapture): on such the second death hath no power, but they shall be priests of God and of Christ, and shall reign with him a thousand years.*

We see here the saints from the first resurrection are to ' *be priests of God and of Christ, and shall reign with him a thousand years.*

Who do they reign over? It certainly isn't the saints from the Tribulation since God has already judged them or they wouldn't have made it to Heaven. Now comes a part I hadn't been taught before.

At the end of the Millennium we are told nations from around the world will come against the great city with a number of who is as the sand of the sea. Where do they come from?

(Zechariah 14:16) [16]*And it shall come to pass, that every one that is left of all the nations which came against Jerusalem shall even go up from year to year to worship the King, the LORD of hosts, and to keep the feast of tabernacles.*

Notice what this prophecy says, '*every one that is left of all the nations which came against Jerusalem*'. Obviously, these nations, that will be left, were not friendly to Israel and the saints. These nations will be around through the entire Millennium. The Book of the Revelation Chapter 19 tells us of the destruction of the army of the antichrist but not their nations.

> (Revelation 19:21) 21 *And the remnant were slain with the sword of him that sat upon the horse, which sword proceeded out of his mouth: and all the fowls were filled with their flesh.*

What we were not told was what became of the nations this army will be from. Apparently, these nations are allowed to continue into the Millennium. They will number as the sand of the sea. This is who the saints will rule and reign over

SATAN IN THE MILLENNIUM

After Armageddon, Satan will be imprisoned in the bottomless pit until the end of the Millennium. At that time he will be released to deceive the nations of the world to come against God one more time.

> (Revelation 20:2-3) 2 *And he laid hold on the dragon, that old serpent, which is the Devil, and Satan, and bound him a thousand years,* 3 *And cast him into the bottomless pit, and shut him up, and set a seal upon him, that he should deceive the nations no more, till the thousand years should be fulfilled: and after that he must be loosed a little season.*

SATAN RELEASED

At the end of the Millennium Satan will be released one last time. In the Book of the Revelation Chapter 20, we see Satan released from his captivity and allowed to go out to deceive the nations from all over the earth and bring them to an apparent second Armageddon.

(Revelation 20:7-9) [7]*And when the thousand years are expired, Satan shall be loosed out of his prison,* [8]*And shall go out to deceive the nations which are in the four quarters of the earth, Gog, and Magog, to gather them together to battle: the number of whom is as the sand of the sea.* [9]*And they went up on the breadth of the earth, and compassed the camp of the saints about and the beloved city: and fire came down from God out of heaven, and devoured them.*

Once again Satan is given an opportunity to try to defeat God. He is released from his prison (the bottomless pit); and is allowed to roam the earth to try and deceive the nations of the earth into attacking the camp of the saints and the beloved city. He is able to gather nations from around the world, Gog and Magog. They bring an army that numbers as the sand of the sea, all for naught. God is able to defeat them without effort.

At this point God has had all of Satan He is going to put up with.

(Revelation 20:10) [10]*And the devil that deceived them was cast into the lake of fire and brimstone, where the beast and the false prophet are, and shall be tormented day and night for ever and ever.*

THE JUDGMENT

The last event of the Millennium is the White Throne Judgment. There seems to be some question as to who goes before this Judgment by Christ.

(Revelation 11:18) [18]*..... the time of the dead, that they should be judged, and that thou shouldest give reward unto thy servants the prophets, and* *to the saints, and them that fear thy name, small and great; and shouldest destroy them which destroy the earth.*

Once again, who has to appear at the judgment? In the Scripture above, the Book of the Revelation 11:18, Jesus says it is time to reward prophets and saints. It is also time to judge the dead and destroy those that destroy the earth. This is a combination of saints and sinners. Here are four Scriptures that make it perfectly clear who is to appear at the judgment.

(Daniel *12:2)* [2]*And many of them that sleep in the dust of the earth shall awake, some to everlasting life, and some to shame and everlasting contempt.*

(Romans 14:10) [10] *But why dost thou judge thy brother? Or why dost thou set at naught thy brother? For we shall all stand before the* ***judgment*** *seat of Christ.*

(2Corinthians 5:10) [10]*For we must all appear before the judgment seat of Christ; that every one may receive the things done in his body, according to that he hath done, whether it be good or bad.*

(Hebrews 9:27) [27]*And as it is appointed unto men once to die, but after this the judgment:*

These Scriptures appear to make it clear that we will all appear before the judgment, saint and sinner. Some of us will be happy and some will not. Those found in the Book of Life will be happy and those not in the Book of Life will not be happy.

(Revelation 20:12) [12] *And I saw the dead, small and great, stand before God; and the books were opened: and another book was opened, which is the book of life: and the dead were judged out of those things which were written in the books, according to their works.*

I thought we weren't to be judged by our works. I thought we had to be in the Book of Life to make it safely through the judgment. We are.

(Acts 20:15) [15]*And whosoever was not found written in the Book of Life was cast into the lake of fire.*

If you are not in the Book of Life your works won't be judged because they are there for a reward. Those in the lake of fire probably won't be getting any rewards.

REMOVAL FROM THE BOOK OF LIFE

Here is another controversial subject. Can you lose your salvation and be removed from the Book of Life? Most religions don't believe you can lose your salvation.

Let's see what Jesus had to say about it.

(Revelation 3:5) [5]*He that overcometh, the same shall be clothed in white raiment; and I will not blot out his name out of the book of life, but I will confess his name before my Father, and before his angels.*

Jesus said '*He that overcometh I will not blot out his name out of the book of life*.' He is implying if you do not overcome, your name can be removed from the Book of Life. If you receive salvation, you get your name in the Book of Life. If you do not overcome the world, your name can be blotted out of the Book of Life. What is meant by overcoming the world? There are two things to consider when you talk about overcoming the world. First are the Ten Commandments. If you break the Ten Commandments and don't repent, you haven't overcome the world. The second is the testimony of Jesus Christ. If you do not maintain your testimony of Jesus Christ you have not overcome the world.

There is another example we can use to depict this in a simple way. The prodigal son is an example of a saved individual and is a member of the family of God. The prodigal son abandoned his family and was lost to his family. He had a choice to make. He was a member of the family, but gave up his relationship with the Family. He could return to his family and share in the security of the family relationship or he could stay away and not share a relationship with his family and its destiny. Fortunately, he decided to return and regain his family relationship and share in its destiny.

If he had stayed away, would he have shared in his family's destiny? There is no indication the family would have gone to find him. It was his choice to stay away or return and seek forgiveness. He chose to return and seek forgiveness and his father welcomed him back in with open arms and much joy. I believe we have the same choice. We know God cannot look upon sin, but we are all sinners. When we sin, we need to repent and ask for forgiveness. For me that is virtually every day. If I die with unrepentant sin, I risk not getting to Heaven.

WORKS

What part do works have at the judgment? I suspect they are more of a part than most people believe. This is another way to possibly lose your salvation.

(James 2:17) 17 *even so faith, if it hath not* ***works****, is dead, being alone.*

James is telling the people, if they receive salvation and then don't do anything they will lose their salvation. If faith is dead, you no longer have the testimony of faith in Jesus Christ. If you don't have that testimony of faith in Jesus Christ you can't be in the Book of Life. If you do not have good works, it appears your name can be blotted out of the Book of Life by God.

Let's look at one more example of works. Jesus told the church at Laodicea their works are neither hot nor cold. Because their works were lukewarm He would spew them out of His mouth. If He spews them out of His mouth, is He going to confess them before His Father? I think not.

> (Revelation 3:14-16) [14]*And unto the angel of the church of the Laodiceans write; These things saith the Amen, the faithful and the true witness, and the beginning of the creation of God;* [15]*I know thy works, that thou art neither cold nor hot; I would thou wet cold or hot.* [16]*So then because thou art lukewarm, and neither cold nor hot, I will spew thee out of my mouth.*
>
> They have not overcome the cares of this world.

Faith

When we speak of Faith and possibly having your name removed from the Book of Life, what do we mean?

> (Luke 17:5-6) [5]*And the apostles said unto the Lord, Increase our faith.* [6]*And the Lord said, If ye had faith as a grain of mustard seed, ye might say unto this sycamore tree, Be thou plucked up by the root, and be thou planted in the sea; and it should obey you.*

Jesus told us in Luke 17:5 where we start. We start with faith as a grain of mustard seed and we could command a tree to be plucked up and it would be. Well, I think we all know it isn't quite that simple.

Let's see if we can understand what he really meant. In Mark 4:31, speaking of faith, Jesus gave us a better understanding of the mustard seed power.

> (Mark 4:31-32) [31]*It is like a grain of mustard seed, which, when it is sown in the earth, is less than all the seeds that be in the earth:* [32]*But when it is sown, it groweth up, and becometh greater than all herbs, and shooteth out great branches; so that the fowls of the air may lodge under the shadow of it.*

Jesus told us the mustard seed is the smallest seed, but it can grow to overshadow the entire garden. What he is saying is, faith must be allowed to grow. If your faith is allowed to grow to maturity, it will have the same power as Jesus Christ. Like any plant in the garden it needs to be nourished and cultivated. How do we cultivate faith? Paul told us one way in Romans 10:17.

> *(Romans 10:17)* [17] *So then faith cometh by hearing, and hearing by the word of God.*

We need to study God's Word. Just reading isn't sufficient. We need to try to understand the application of His Word to our lives, to our friends and the world. We need to be able to see as God sees. The more we study His Word, the closer we will get to being able to pluck that tree.

If we decide not to nourish and cultivate our faith, we will fall back to our old ways and lose our testimony and our salvation. Jesus spoke of this in the parable of the sower.

(Matthew 13:18-23) [18]*Hear ye therefore the parable of the sower.* [19]*When any one heareth the word of the kingdom, and understandeth it not, then cometh the wicked one, and catcheth away that which was sown in his heart. This is he which received seed by the way side.* [20]*But he that received the seed into stony places, the same is he that heareth the word, and anon with joy receiveth it;* [21]*Yet hath he not root in himself, but dureth for a while: for when tribulation or persecution ariseth because of the word, by and by he is offended.* [22]*He also that received seed among the thorns is he that heareth the word; and the care of this world, and the deceitfulness of riches, choke the word, and he becometh unfruitful.* [23]*But he that received seed into the good ground is he that heareth the word, and understandeth it; which also beareth fruit, and bringeth forth, some an hundredfold, some sixty, some thirty.*

This parable covers the person saved in a moment and then their passion fades and rests in the belief once saved always saved no matter what. Compare that person to the one that brings much fruit. The last person has taken that first passion and grown in faith over time and has become a witness for Jesus Christ.

The condition of your soul when you die is what you will be judged by. If it is dark with sin, you will be in serious trouble.

Those in the Book of Life and having good works will have rewards for their good works.

(Matthew 16:27) [27]*For the Son of man shall come in the glory of his Father with his angels; and then he shall reward every man according to his works.*

(Revelation 22:12) [12]*And, behold, I come quickly; and my reward is with me, to give every man according as his work shall be.*

Here is the best description of the Great White Throne Judgment I have found.

> (Matthew 13:41-50) [41]*The Son of man shall send forth his angels, and they shall gather out of his kingdom all things that offend, and them which do iniquity;* [42]*And shall cast them into a furnace of fire: there shall be wailing and gnashing of teeth.* [43]*Then shall the righteous shine forth as the sun in the kingdom of their Father. Who hath ears to hear, let him hear.* [44]*Again, the kingdom of heaven is like unto treasure hid in a field; the which when a man hath found, he hideth, and for joy thereof goeth and selleth all that he hath, and buyeth that field.* [45]*Again, the kingdom of heaven is like unto a merchant man, seeking goodly pearls:* [46]*Who, when he had found one pearl of great price, went and sold all that he had, and bought it.* [47]*Again, the kingdom of heaven is like unto a net, that was cast into the sea, and gathered of every kind:* [48]*Which, when it was full, they drew to shore, and sat down, and gathered the good into vessels, but cast the bad away.* [49]*So shall it be at the end of the world: the angels shall come forth, and sever the wicked from among the just,* [50]*And shall cast them into the furnace of fire: there shall be wailing and gnashing of teeth.*

> (Revelation 20:11) [11]*And I saw a great white throne, and him that sat on it, from whose face the earth and the heaven fled away; and there was found no place for them.*

It says here, the earth and Heaven fled away. Where did they go and when did they go? The Scripture doesn't say.

NEW HEAVEN AND NEW EARTH

Once the judgment is over and Satan has been cast into the lake of fire, we see Heaven opened up. Then a new Heaven and a new earth arrive. When the judgment is complete, all things will become new.

(Revelation 21:1) [1]*And I saw a new heaven and a new earth: for the first heaven and the first earth were passed away; and there was no more sea.*

Where did the old Heaven and old earth go? How do we go from the old earth to the new earth? We aren't given any information on how this takes place. My suspicion is they are simply remade by God. That's only a guess and it really isn't important. God is in control and he'll make it happen whatever way it goes.

NEW JERUSALEM

Once we are on the new earth, we will see a New Jerusalem coming down out of Heaven.

(Revelation 21:2) [2]*And I John saw the holy city, New Jerusalem, coming down from God out of heaven, prepared as a bride adorned for her husband.*

We need to go way back for this one. Jesus said He would prepare a place for us. Over the years we have been told we are going to enter through the pearly gates and we will walk the golden streets in Heaven. Jesus said, in John 14, He is going to prepare a place for us. At the same time He said He will come again and receive us unto Him.

(John 14:1-3) [1]*Let not your heart be troubled: ye believe in God, believe also in me.* [2]*In my Father's house are many mansions: if it were not so, I would have told you. I go to prepare a place for you. .* [3]*And if I go and prepare a place for you, I will come again, and receive you unto myself; that where I am, there ye may be also.*

Well, I'm sorry but when we walk through the pearly gates, it won't be in Heaven. Those pearly gates will be on earth (or a new earth). He said, '*that where I am, there ye may be also.*' He won't be in Heaven at that time. He will be on earth.

> (Revelation 21:3-5) [3]*And I heard a great voice out of heaven saying, Behold, the tabernacle of God is with men, and he will dwell with them, and they shall be his people, and God himself shall be with them, and be their God.* [4]*And God shall wipe away all tears from their eyes; and there shall be no more death, neither sorrow, nor crying, neither shall there be any more pain: for the former things are passed away.* [5]*And he that sat upon the throne said, Behold, I make all things new. And he said unto me, Write: for these words are true and faithful.*

This is the culmination of all we have been through. We have arrived at eternity. God is on the throne amongst His people. No more ruling by remote control. We will be able to look Him in the face and speak with Him face to face.

> (Revelation 21:6-7) [6]*And he said unto me, it is done. I am Alpha and Omega, the beginning and the end. I will give unto him that is athirst of the fountain of the water of life freely.* [7]*He that overcometh shall inherit all things; and I will be his God and he shall be my son.*

No more sin, no more pain or sorrow or hunger or fear or heat or cold. Welcome to Paradise.

> (Revelation 21:8) [8]*But the fearful, and unbelieving, and the abominable, and murderers, and whoremongers, and sorcerers, and idolaters, and all liars, shall have their part in the lake which burneth with fire and brimstone: which is the second death.*

If you want to read about this glorious city, you can read about it in the Book of the Revelation 21:10-22:5.

One thing about the city you may not understand in reading about it. The size of the city is difficult to comprehend in Bible measurements. It is 1500 miles long, 1500 miles wide and 1500 miles high. The wall around the city is approximately 216 ft high.

Not everyone that makes it to eternity will reside in the city. There will be nations of saved people that reside in the light of it and will have continuous access to the city.

> (Revelation 21:24-27) 24 *And the nations of them which are saved shall walk in the light of it: and the kings of the earth do bring their glory and honour into it.* 25 *And the gates of it shall not be shut at all by day: for there shall be no night there.* 26 *And they shall bring the glory and honour of the nations into it.* 27 *And there shall in no wise enter into it any thing that defileth, neither whatsoever worketh abomination, or maketh a lie: but they which are written in the Lamb's book of life.*

The Book of the Revelation was written as God commanded and it will come true for those that keep the sayings of the prophecy as stated in the Book of the Revelation 22:6.

> (Revelation 22:6-7) 6 *And he said unto me, 'these sayings are faithful and true: and the Lord God of the holy prophets sent his angel to show unto his servants the things which must shortly be done'.* 7 *Behold, I come quickly: blessed is he that keepeth the sayings of the prophecy of this book.*

CPSIA information can be obtained at www.ICGtesting.com
Printed in the USA
241006LV00003B/33/P